More Praise for G[illegible]

"*Gospel Discipleship* helped me as the pastor identify as a Markan figuring out strategies for ministry with a Lukan church. When a leader is not of the same type as the church, it can seem frustrating to attain a deeper relationship and commitment with Christ. Because of this resource, we simplified our leadership structure and reimagined our vision and mission statement so that relational Lukans can get into ministry with each other more easily."

—George Odell, pastor, First UMC of Clinton, Clinton, AR

"*Gospel Discipleship* moved my church from inertia (staring at each other in meetings) to finally learning how to work together to create our church's discipleship pathway. We were also able to use individual results to be sure there is a balance on our administrative teams. Our staff also realized how to communicate with each other based on their discipleship pathway. Our staff team has never been stronger!"

—Jeanne Williams, senior pastor, First UMC, Bella Vista, AR

"*Gospel Discipleship* is a wonderful resource for the journey of growing into the image of Christ. The author brings a fresh perspective and even a new language to the ancient practice of discipleship. Readers are able to learn more about themselves and gain new insight into how those around them best grow as disciples."

—Ken Willard, Professional Certified Coach; Director of Discipleship, Leadership, and Congregational Vitality, West Virginia Conference, UMC; author, *Stride*

"*Gospel Discipleship* offers a fresh, creative approach found nowhere else—and has great potential to help both individuals and congregations better understand and own their unique pathways for spiritual growth. I look forward to recommending this to pastors and leaders who long to finally bring discipleship into new clarity for those they shepherd."

—Sue Nilson Kibbey, church consultant; author, *Ultimate Reliance: Breakthrough Prayer Practices for Leaders*

"The bridge has been blown! For most people, the twenty-first-century church is inaccessible. The only way to meet challenge in a post-Christian world is to identify disciples who make disciples. *Gospel Discipleship* built that bridge. *Gospel Discipleship* can truly thrive in any congregation."

—Michael Beck, pastor, Wildwood UMC, Wildwood, FL; author, *A Field Guide to Methodist Fresh Expressions*

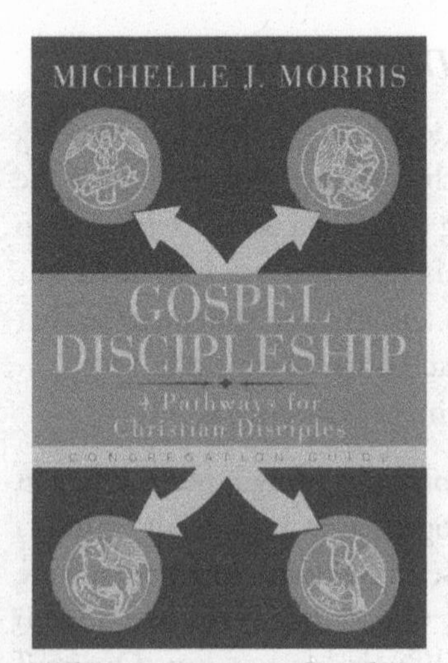

Congregation Guide
ISBN 9781501899072

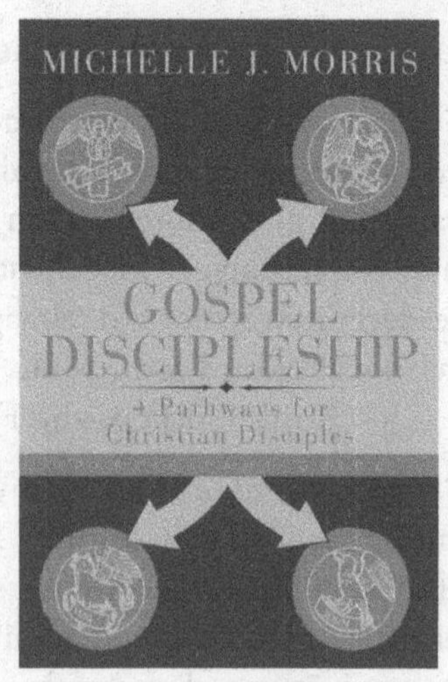

Participant Guide
ISBN 9781501899058

Streaming Videos

ISBN 9781791008260

ISBN 9781791008277

ISBN 9781791008284

ISBN 9781791008291

ISBN 9781791008307

ISBN 9781791008314

Gospel Discipleship Assessment
www.ministrymatters.com/gospeldiscipleship

MICHELLE J. MORRIS

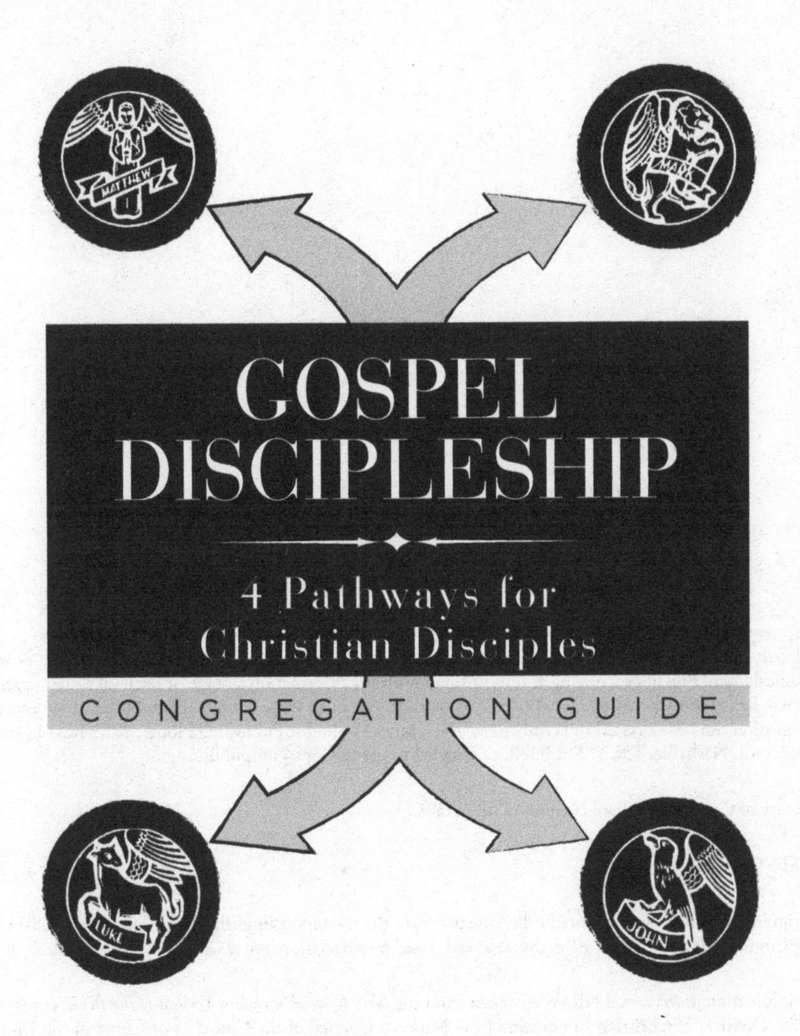

Abingdon Press
Nashville

GOSPEL DISCIPLESHIP CONGREGATION GUIDE:
4 PATHWAYS FOR CHRISTIAN DISCIPLES

Library of Congress Control Number: 2020933042

ISBN: 978-1-5018-9907-2

20 21 22 23 24 25 26 27 28 29—10 9 8 7 6 5 4 3 2 1
MANUFACTURED IN THE UNITED STATES OF AMERICA

CONTENTS

ACKNOWLEDGMENTS

I am deeply grateful to the Arkansas Conference of The United Methodist Church for their role in this project. I am particularly grateful to Bishop Gary Mueller for his vision of discipleship, and the Center for Vitality team, Rev. Dede Roberts and Cathy Hall, who encouraged and championed this work. I am also blessed to have been able to collaborate with the Center for Communications under the phenomenal leadership of Amy Ezell.

This work is stronger thanks in large part to the incredible talents at Abingdon Press. I could not be more thankful to work with such an amazing group of people.

Several congregations were brave and bold enough to let me test out this process on them. They are the source of the vast majority of learning that shapes this congregation guide. While I am still working with congregations and still learning, these first few churches and their pastors will be near and dear to my heart for their generosity and spirit of adventure. They are all in various stages of implementing discipleship systems (many of them are Lukan congregations that are slow to change and need significant buy-in before adoption will work), but they have all certainly contributed to my understanding of discipleship in powerful ways. With one noted exception, all these churches are located in Arkansas.

I begin with a church that is in many ways the bookends of this grand experiment, First United Methodist Church of Clinton (pastor Rev. George Odell, layperson Bryan Ayres is in the Markan video). I received the revelation for this process from the Holy Spirit on February 20, 2019. I happened to have a meeting about discipleship scheduled with the Clinton leadership on February 24. I asked each of the leaders there three questions about discipleship. Following that discussion, I explained a rough idea of Gospel Discipleship, and then said, "If I am right, based on your answers to these questions, you are a Lukan congregation." I then convinced them to distribute an assessment to the congregation. They worked it into their year, and in October 2019 I returned to share their results. They are, in fact, Lukan. I met for the second time with their leadership on the same day I sent the draft manuscripts to Abingdon to start the editorial process. Clinton will always be at the heart of this experience for me.

First UMC of Charleston (Rev. Daniel Thueson) integrated this work into a weekend training on discipleship for church leaders, and gave me an opportunity to test out usefulness of my presentation. Alma and Kibler UMCs (Rev. Doug Phillips) gave me insight into a two-point charge, and how to think through charges that are yoked but are different primary discipleship types. Vilonia UMC (Rev. James Kjorlaug) gave significant time and space for training, were incredibly involved during my presentation and provided significant examples that made their way into both books thanks to their willingness to engage. Vilonia also allowed deep reflection on how a pastor and church with different types can learn to work effectively together. I also noted in the participant guide how integral both Doug at Alma and Kibler and James at Vilonia have been in collaborating and supporting me throughout this process, and part of their contribution comes from the congregations that they lead.

First UMC of Bella Vista (Revs. Jeanne Williams and Brenda Wideman) was my first larger size church to participate on a broad scale. Rev. Williams invited me to work with church leadership, staff, and then the congregation at large, allowing reflection and experimentation on how understanding our discipleship impacts how we work together.

Marshall Presbyterian Church of Marshall, NC (Rev. Melissa Upchurch and layperson Carol Brown) represented my first non-United

Methodist, non-Arkansas church. I particularly enjoyed reflecting on the results with Carol, who works with her church specifically around discipleship and education.

St. Paul Maumelle (Rev. Lavon Post) and First UMC of Sheridan (Rev. Todd-Paul Taulbee) were my first two potential two-type churches, and are still working through what a hybrid model of discipleship looks like. Oak Forest UMC in Little Rock (Revs. Jana Green and Trinette Barnes) danced with the possibility of a difference in church leadership types and overall church types. St. Luke, a campus of Pulaski Heights UMC in Little Rock (Rev. Andreá Cummings), provided an opportunity to reflect on how this process could define discipleship for a new church or church relaunch. The New Heights service of Pulaski Heights UMC (Rev. Betsy Singleton Snyder) added work with small groups to the conversation. Magazine, Paris, and Waveland (Rev. Judy Hall) showed how this process could be integrated as a small group study and sermon series to revitalize discipleship in a church. And First UMC of Newport (Rev. Jeremy Pressgrove) tested out another training model and ended up confirming the validity of these types in the process.

Some congregations have not been part of Gospel Discipleship, but were part of the work that led up to this model. These include First UMC of Rector (Rev. Jacob Lynn), Wesley UMC of Conway (Rev. Patti Butler), St. Paul UMC of Searcy (Rev. Judy Rudd), and St. Paul UMC of Fort Smith (Rev. Steve Poarch).

Finally, I am grateful to all the churches who have shaped me and helped me understand discipleship. So thank you, Foundery UMC (formerly Lowell, AR), Elm Springs UMC, and St. Andrew UMC in Plano, TX, for training me as a disciple. And thank you especially for the ones who trained me as a pastor: First UMC of Hurst, TX, First UMC of West Memphis, AR, and Cavanaugh and Wesley UMCs in Fort Smith. You have all blessed me more than you will ever know, and you are part of this book as you continue to shape my journey to this day.

And to my family, especially my husband Travis and son Soren, I am always thankful for your love and support. My love to you all.

INTRODUCTION

- A pastor rearranged the sanctuary seating without telling anyone he was going to do so, and people were actually happy about it.
- A church with a history of fighting with each other suddenly realized it wasn't personal; they just have different understandings of discipleship.
- A committee that had spent a year developing a mission and vision for their church, only to watch no one buy in, realized why that happened.
- A nominations committee had clarity about who should serve on which committees, and why.
- A leadership group preparing to relaunch a congregation realized they had the perfect mix of people to be welcoming to everyone in their neighborhood.
- A staff member understood why mass emails to people in her congregation rarely resulted in getting volunteers.
- A pastor realized if he made time to visit with his leadership before they started talking business, they would get so much more done.

These are a few of the results witnessed in pilot churches participating in the Gospel Discipleship process, which provides an on-ramp for pointing each follower of Jesus in the right direction. With rare exceptions, training in Gospel Discipleship results in a congregation actually making a significant turn toward fruitful discipleship. These results are nothing short of miraculous. As a pastor, you live for those moments. As a guest teacher, you rarely expect to see them, figuring you are planting seeds. Yet the transformation, while not complete, is immediate.

Part of the transformation occurs simply because this process gives people a vocabulary for discipleship, and it is a vocabulary they readily pick up because it is anchored in scripture. Church people resist fitting into corporate models or they are skeptical of business jargon imposed on spiritual behaviors. They long for something that feels authentic and distinct to our faith.

Most people actually don't know what it means to be a disciple. We have thrown that word around in such generic ways that people can't really grasp what it means for their lives. They know it roughly means following Jesus, and they can usually identify times in their lives when they have felt like they have done that, but they have been rather haphazard about it. They have certainly not been intentional, because for too long the church hasn't been intentional about showing them how.

Perhaps many aging churches in hindsight have struggled to sustain the meaning of discipleship. This Gospel Discipleship experience will help your church overcome the struggle. First, Gospel Discipleship will identify your *who*. Who you are, individually and collectively, affects how you will live your discipleship. Once you understand your *who*, you can make a plan for *how*. That allows you to live into your *why*, which is to live a life dedicated to Christ. It's a joy to see participants excited about putting a system in place to live it out! When someone tags you on social media because an energized disciple has found an article and she says, "Would be perfect for our Lukan friends," then they are getting it. When their vocabulary is changed, it is not long before their actions and lives are changed. Our hope for you and your people is that you experience a revival of discipleship by going through this process, and above all that it helps you make even more disciples, because we finally understand who we are and how to live that out for Christ.

Using This Congregation Guide with the Participant Guide

Before reading further, take the test online (or the version included at the end of this book) and then read the *Gospel Discipleship Participant Guide* (ISBN 9781501899058) to understand your Gospel type. The *Participant Guide* is the source for interpreting the discipleship traits of each of the four types. Each leader and each participant needs a copy of the *Participant Guide* (which includes a copy of the test for those who don't choose to take it online). The interpretations in the *Participant Guide*—for Markans, Mattheans, Lukans, and Johannines—anchor and validate Gospel Discipleship in the Bible.

To remain consistent with the *Participant Guide*, Markan types come before Matthean ones. This is a different order than found in the Bible, but it lines up with the order that the Gospels were written. For more about this chronology, see the *Participant Guide*.

Who Do We Test, and How?

Since launching this discipleship approach, the question recurring often from pastors or leaders initiating this system in their churches is "Who do we test?" followed quickly by "How do we test them?"

Who you test in your congregation is the first step, and how you get them to agree to the process is the second step. The first step depends upon your aims for establishing a discipleship pathway, which also depends on your context. For instance, if you are part of a congregation who historically does well with congregation-wide studies or has had success with spiritual gifts assessments, getting the whole congregation to participate in this process will probably be relatively straightforward. If you have had a recent negative experience with such work, however, you may be met with skepticism. In that case, you may want to test a key group of leaders and experiment on a small scale before you try to roll it out to the whole church. During testing of this process, most of the churches have had mixed or frustrated results with church-wide or regional programs in circulation. They've become skeptical toward "another conference program" or a megachurch book study, because they don't think it will take their context into account. If this is your experience, try testing a small group to see how it works and then imagine the possibilities for an entire congregation.

Furthermore, the passion and confidence of the leaders who seek to use this approach will also determine its success.

Here are some experiences from test churches, which can help estimate a similar circumstance for your own context.

Two-point church charge with different discipleship types. One pastor with two churches initially tested one of his churches because he recognized they were in different places in their ministry journey. After he tested the first church, however, he realized that he was actually misreading the other church's discipleship type. Perhaps it had a different Gospel type than the first, so he worked on testing both. He distributed the test to as many in the congregation as he could get, but they were distributed differently, which actually reflected the pastor's intuition and knowledge about the churches. He distributed it by hand, electronically, and in the newsletter to one church (the church that tested Matthean, which meant that multiple entry points were wise) and by hand to the other church (which ended up being Lukan—so the personal touch was wise too). When we shared the results, we largely had the tests from the key leaders at the Matthean church, and when asked if they wanted to push for the whole congregation to take the test, they didn't see a need. They wanted to move right to action, and because they have a critical mass and the leaders of action behind the process, it worked out. The other church had a mix of people return tests, and while they did agree that they probably are Lukan, they wanted some time to reflect on if they wanted to push for the whole congregation to take the test. They don't want to leave anyone out, and it needed more conversation. That is a very Lukan approach.

A church that runs everything through a committee. The pastor had someone on staff who is in charge of Christian education, so she delegated the process to the CE director, but only after she had the blessings of her board. The Christian education pastor is careful about what goes out to all the people, so she was hesitant to take it to the whole church. This church is also in a different denomination than the Gospel Discipleship developers, so hesitation about identity formation was prudent. The CE director decided a Sunday school class would be a good place to experiment. If that class feels the experience is worthwhile, they will lead the pathways into the whole church.

"Church" within a church. This community is a worship service within the context of a larger church. The distinctive worship service is struggling with its sense of community in light of recent challenges in the denomination. The lead pastor of the distinct worship group used this Gospel Discipleship process to guide conversations about identity in tandem with the launch of some small groups that should strengthen the sense of community. She distributed the assessment during worship, and then reflected on the results in subsequent worship events, and in a follow-up session. She thinks this process will give the worship service a renewed sense of community and shared vocabulary for talking about and acting on their discipleship.

Church getting ready to build a new sanctuary. This church is in the midst of intentional reflection on present identity and who they need to be to reach more people. They would like their space to reflect those realities. This discipleship assessment will be a tool in that building process, primarily one that helps define who they are. The assessment was shared with everyone in the church willing to take it, and the results will be discussed in a Sunday afternoon workshop. They will deliberately look at how their corporate discipleship type can be reflected in a worship space.

New church start. A new church start was going to start out organized as small groups in homes. The pastor had her key group of leaders take the assessment, then they did some deep work on what each type meant. Each small group would have an emphasis on the type that the host leader exhibited. They would think in terms of mission emphases that met those types, as well as deciding whether they would look more like spaces for holy friendship, active study, faith mentoring, or creative outlets. New people who were not invited to specific groups by a friend would be tested and then a group or groups would be recommended to them based on their type. People who were invited directly into a group would still be tested, and if their type did not match that group but they wanted to stay with people they knew, that would be fine. They would be encouraged to bring a different take on things to their group, to consider switching groups, or perhaps to start their own group once their comfort level grew.

Sunday school class. Some of the individuals who tested the assessment were fascinated by the results and found them useful. They also could see applicability for their Sunday school class. First, they found it would be a good conversation piece among the people in the group, and give them a new frame for discussing discipleship. They also, however, could use dominant types to consider what they might do additionally as a group. For instance, classes that tested high as Mattheans added a mission component to their time together. Lukans had a better understanding of why they all like to get together and have dinner, but it also helped them understand how they had become cliquish. As for process, Sunday school classes easily took the assessment during one of their classes, and they emailed the people who were missing. They then spent the next couple of weeks assessing what the results meant for them.

Church that is "spinning its wheels." One church recognizes that it can't get any traction. They are stuck in a rut. Everyone is going through the motions. They had tried some church-wide emphases, and those had flopped. Leaders recognize the potential of this assessment to help them head off things that would not work for them, as well as better identify things that would work, but they also face a weary group of folks. So the leaders are starting with themselves. They plan to use the resultant understanding to transform how their governing board works. The aim is to build a small success and some enthusiasm, and then ease the congregation into the process later.

Church working on its vision statement. One church had a pastor who had been with them a few years. He had built up trust with the people. He recognized that it was time the church revisit its old vision statement. He began the conversations about vision in tandem with a talk about discipleship. The aim is that the vision of the church can better reflect the disciples they are called and equipped to be. He also recognizes, however, that as a United Methodist pastor he is not likely to be at that church much longer. He asked a significant lay leader to help encourage the whole church to participate in the assessment and to lead the discussion around vision so that it is the church's vision and does not die when the pastor is moved. The two of them distributed the assessment, and then spent a couple of months coaxing them back from each person. Turns out, that was a great move because this church is Lukan, so now all of the people feel part of the process as they unfold their new vision.

Church working on an intentional discipleship system. The majority of churches tested were working on designing their discipleship system. This objective is a widespread trend in US congregation across the denominations. Pastors worked through this process in various ways. One held a weekend discipleship seminar after distributing the assessment to the whole church and folded this work into the larger conversation of what constitutes discipleship. A pastor of a large church worked with the Sunday school classes to get each one to go through the process, because the strength of that church's community was in its Sunday school. One pastor distributed the assessment to key people who made up her discipleship team, and then tracked if there were any varieties in types based on which worship service people attended. She also tested her staff and used the results to cultivate conversation among the staff about discipleship, as they would be central in helping implement the church's discipleship system.

These are the primary ways congregations use and adapt this system for their context. As you reflect on your own situation, you may find an analogy in one of these options, or you may get creative and go off script. If you are a pastor or a church leader, and you would really like to encourage all of your people (or at least as many of them as you can) and you can roughly guess what the lead type will be in your congregation, then lean into that type to get it done. For Mattheans, make it an action they all do together. Mattheans would probably do well having it handed out during worship, and then followed up as homework. For Markans, frame it as a spiritual gifts test for what kind of disciple you are. Help them to understand it will identify how they are gifted by the Spirit for discipleship. For Lukans, the personal touch is going to matter. You may need to directly ask as many people as possible, and help each one understand how important it is that each person be part of this process so they can know how to better build relationships with God, each other, and the community. As for a Johannine church, just make sure your pastor and key leaders push it out. The backing of authority should be enough to get people behind the process.

Between the reflections on how different types will respond to taking the assessment and the examples shared, you will have a sense of who you can or should test, and how you could go about doing it. If none of these situations seem to fit, though, pray and reflect about how self-awareness in your congregation can grow by understanding that followers of Jesus had diverse strengths when deepening their confidence and hope in God's reign on earth. Of course, you can invite your key leaders into the conversation as well. Even if you have a few assessments, you know more about your coworkers than you knew before, and it becomes a place to begin conversation.

Where Do You Find the Test?

You may have decided who you need to test and how, but now you need to do the Gospel Discipleship assessment. If you are taking it as a group or a church, you can go to www.MinistryMatters.com/gospeldiscipleship

and take the test online. The test will calculate an individual's Gospel type and email the result, along with a description of each person's discipleship type. If you prefer not to take the test online, a copy is found in the *Participant Guide*, with direction on how to tabulate your own Gospel type.

Implementing Gospel Discipleship Church-Wide

Before Week 1: Hand out the *Gospel Discipleship Participant Guide* to the adult small group(s) at your church.

- Preview a four- or five-week topical worship series on Gospel Discipleship.
- Have participant guides available for distribution to the worship participants.
- Invite all to attend an adult small group during the church-wide study.
- Play the video trailer in worship for Gospel Discipleship.
- See the customizable order of worship for each week found at www.gospeldiscipleship.net.
- Gather a small group of leaders weekly to engage in Gospel Discipleship strategic thinking implications. Give each a copy of this Congregational Guide.
- See www.gospeldiscipleship.net for additional suggestions, including tactics for collecting the individual assessments from each participant.
- Week 1: Sermon on Markan Discipleship
- Week 2: Sermon on Matthean Discipleship
- Week 3: Sermon on Lukan Discipleship

- Week 4: Sermon on Johannine Discipleship
- Week 4 or 5: Worship: What Kind of Disciples Are We Together?
- Reveal primary and secondary discipleship types to congregation (the highest number of Gospel Discipleship types).
- Share insights from the Gospel Discipleship strategic thinking group of leaders.

Using This Congregation Guide

Unlike the *Participant Guide*, which is organized by discipleship type, this guide is organized by six topics, such as intentional discipleship for a church of your type, or worship in a church of each type. The consideration revolves around how this guide will likely be used. A church may want to try some of these adjustments, or roll them out bit by bit. The reason all the types are gathered together under the topics is that most churches, even if they lean into their primary type, will need to understand the realities of the other types, because you have the other types in your congregation. As with most thoughts about diversity, the most anxiety pertaining to Gospel Discipleship concerns the inclusion of people who fall in the nondominant type at a church. First, regularly assure the participants that a church cannot be the strong Markan or Matthean or Lukan or Johannine church without the presence of the other types, who will keep the whole moving forward in your discipleship. The metaphor of the "the body of Christ" found in 1 Corinthians is a familiar way to teach that God makes us different on purpose. Then discuss the section on how to integrate the other types into congregations. Any type can live into their discipleship by using any of the four systems. Check out www.gospeldiscipleship.net to see if there are recommendations there, or submit your scenario or problem to the author at the website and we will work through it together.

Chapter One

INTENTIONAL DISCIPLESHIP AS A CHURCH OF YOUR TYPE

When you have tallied all your tests and figured out what type of church you are, then the goal is to create an explicit way for you to live your discipleship together. Once you've defined the predominant discipleship type in your church, it is more clearly apparent for people who come to visit your church. Guests, visitors, and seekers are much more interested in a faith community that is open about how they live out their discipleship.

Most churches have collectively forgotten how to be disciples. Perhaps when Christianity was a dominant force throughout the culture, some churches didn't teach about discipleship, because it was being reinforced as an identity or affiliation in our everyday lives. So we neglected intentional faith formation, and people forgot how to share it. We cannot take for granted that the people who sit in the pews know how to be a disciple.

Think of it this way. Imagine the most beautiful lake you will ever see on the other side of a forest. To view it would literally take your breath away. However, the forest is a wall of trees. The brush is so dense that no light is breaking through. Thorn bushes cover the ground under the trees. How motivated are you going to be to see that lake? You are probably going to just say, "No thanks. I bet there is a picture of it on the web somewhere. I will just look at that." But what if, instead of a tangle of brush, there was a clearly cut, straight path that leads to the lake? Now you would probably be more motivated to go.

When people come into our church for the first time, too often we are pointing to a tangled forest. Actually, too often we are just pushing them in the forest, with no explanation about why we just did that. We need to cut the path that leads to God's saving grace. We need people to see the destination, and to see how to get there. We need it for the visitor. And we need it for us.

How do we figure out how to live our discipleship together? The first step is to figure out who we are, which is done by taking the assessment together. Your Gospel types suggest a particular discipleship system. Once we know the primary pattern for *who* we are as a church, the *how* becomes so much clearer. The *Participant Guide* spells out a basic frame for individuals, and that frame will be the basis of the system built for a whole church, so be sure you have access to that description. As a church looks at building a system, however, we will also look at how to communicate it through images, as well as other elements a church wants to introduce to synthesize your discipleship.

Catching Fire: Markan Intentional Discipleship

- **Discipleship System:** Spiritual Gifts Empowerment
- **Additional Elements:** Discernment team, prayer team, spiritual gifts counselors, simplified governing structure
- **Communicative Image:** Fire, fireworks

In the *Participant Guide*, we learned that an individual's discipleship plan would revolve around discerning her gifts and then utilizing those gifts in the areas of spiritual growth, worship, service, and witness. The same will hold true for a church-wide Markan discipleship system. In a truly egalitarian way, one that takes into account how each individual contributes to the whole, a Markan church should start by testing the individuals. Since this does rely on individuals freely sharing their results with those in the church who are organizing the system, you need to be transparent about the purpose of such sharing. It may also mean that church leadership should share their results with the congregation as this system begins to unfold. This is especially true because Markans tend to be suspicious of systems, and particularly suspicious of anything that smacks of the programmatic approach of organized religion. Help the people see that in fact it is giving voice to the reality that understanding each individual helps the church better understand who they are as a whole.

The key to a Markan discipleship system is to have everyone take a spiritual gifts test. This corporate assessment of spiritual gifts is a distinct follow-up after the Gospel Discipleship survey identified your church's dominant pattern as Markan. A well-known and effective spiritual gifts survey can be found at https://www.ministrymatters.com/all/entry/4640/spiritual-gifts-discovering-and-using. The first time the church undergoes this process, you will use the results to put your Markan infrastructure in place (while acknowledging that Markans aren't fans of infrastructure, but this one is Spirit centered so it should be acceptable). So a Markan church applies the first round of spiritual gifts tests to empower people to use their gifts. The learning from this inventory of gifts may lead to a complete reorganization of the church ministry teams, so be bold and do it anyway. At one new church start, we did a church-wide spiritual gifts test when we were headed into our fourth year of existence. After scoring the tests we were shocked see all twenty-five gifts represented in our seventy-member church, but nearly everyone was serving in the wrong capacity. Instead of being intentional from the beginning by matching people with their strengths and our needs, we had stuck people in slots as they joined. However, we chose not to reorganize our efforts to match the gifts, and we closed in less than two years.

When you assess everyone's gifts, you are looking for a few particular types of gifts. One set includes those who have gifts of discernment, creativity, wisdom, and prophecy or visioning. These folks need to serve on whatever entity you have that does the strategic thinking for the church, and then empowers people to live into their vision. Markans are not huge fans of mission and vision statements. Missional slogans are too confining; Markans yearn to adjust to the Spirit as conditions change. However, without some strategic thinking for the church, Markans can be susceptible to missing the will of the Spirit. A Markan faith community needs balance. First, the mission of the church can be a solid stake in the ground: make disciples who follow Jesus. The strategic decisions for how that happens in a particular place, time, and with particular people is what Markans aim to change. The rate of change in our world now means that most churches should review their strategic thinking for making disciples every two to four years. Markans, however, may want to look at an annual vision. How do they determine the vision? The strategic thinkers look at two primary things: the gifts of the people in the church, and the needs and desires of the community in which they sit. Where those two things intersect, that is the vision. Then, with that vision in place, the leadership gives permission to disciples who come forward with energy to use their gifts for the benefit of the community in ways that make sense.

Those who have counseling and teaching gifts should be asked to serve as the shepherds of the church's discipleship process. These people will meet with any new people ready to integrate into the life of the church. They administer the Gospel Discipleship test followed by the spiritual gifts test. Simply send an email out to new folks with a link to the tests, and then follow up with a request to share results with the counselor. These counselors should meet with anyone who is tested to review their results and help them map out a plan for growing in their discipleship based on their gifts. They should also share the results with the strategic thinking team and the prayer team to include new people in their work. This team should also hold the whole church accountable to regularly retake the spiritual gifts test. We know that the Spirit will lift up different gifts among us as the seasons change. Testing again every few years allows us to stay attentive to God's will.

Everyone in a Markan church learns to pray for the work of the church. However, Markan churches also need to look for those with a gift for prayer and healing in their midst. Those who are so gifted should be tapped as a prayer team. This team should be in regular communication with both the counselors and with the strategic thinking team. They should intentionally pray for all the efforts of the church, and all the disciples in the church, as well as for the community around them. And those with healing capacities should be praying for and envisioning the bold, boundary-breaking possibilities of aligning with the Spirit.

Ideally, these three teams are all that would be required for Markan governance. The strategic thinking team would handle division of the budget, since that would be how the vision or plan is implemented. Once people are empowered into their roles, they should be relatively self-regulating and self-perpetuating as new people are identified with similar gifts. However, denominations have particular requirements for governance, so it is important to meet those requirements (which Markans tend to resist). If your denomination requires a cluster of committees, then at least be intentional about who serves on them; make sure their gifts match up with the purpose of the committee. However, if your denomination allows for simplification of structure, Markan churches should definitely do that! Markans do not like to be hampered by complicated church governance. Clear the way for the agility of the Spirit. It is a necessity for Markans.

Images are important for communicating an understanding of your discipleship pathway. Each path described here has some widely applicable images, though of course you can imagine other images that resonate with your church and context. For Markans, fire would be the dominant image for Holy Spirit–driven discipleship. Even more than a flame, though, exploding fireworks might be the best image for the discipleship of a Markan church, because it starts from a central explosion and radiates out.

Fireworks can represent an individual's journey, with the newly discovered gifts at the center, and then the ways of expressing the realms of discipleship radiating out. This same image can be used for the whole church, with the year's vision at the center and the ways of living into discipleship in support of that vision exploding out. Markan churches who live into their gifts and then give those gifts to their community can't help but catch fire with God's energy and movement.

Steps for Implementing a Markan Discipleship Pathway

1. Have the whole church take a spiritual gifts test. You can use one you know about already, or find one here: https://www.ministrymatters.com/all/entry/4640/spiritual-gifts-discovering-and-using.

2. When using the results, determine who should serve on your discernment team, prayer team, and as spiritual gifts counselors. Train each of the teams for their work.

3. The discernment team studies results of the whole church and mission field; determines potential intersections; and casts the strategic direction for the church each year.

4. The strategic direction is shared with the congregation, individuals are given their spiritual gifts results (if they haven't obtained them already) and counseled or encouraged to identify ways they can plug into the strategies.

5. Individuals are given instructions for creating their own individual pathway to grow in their discipleship. Individuals are also encouraged to bring forward new ideas for serving the vision.

6. Other aspects of church life are aligned with Markan discipleship (e.g., work on simplifying governing structure, worship can be assessed, and programs assessed for alignment with the strategies expressed by the vision).

7. Process for integrating new people is spelled out (take gifts test, meet with spiritual gifts counselor) and a plan is laid out for individual discipleship through counseling sessions.

8. Regular review of church ministries and of the strategic vision (annually) and regular testing of individuals to ascertain whether people are serving in ways that make sense for their gifts.

On the Right Path: Matthean Discipleship

- **Discipleship System:** Charting Your Path
- **Additional Elements:** Simplified governing structure, strategic thinking (vision) team, mission team
- **Communicative Image:** Charts, paths, anything that marks a journey from beginning to end

Mattheans find that implementing a discipleship system is very appealing! They will also find a plethora of available resources to put one in place, because Mattheans develop clear systems that are easy to share (and write about).

By building off the work from the participant guide, a Matthean church thinks holistically about discipleship. Instead of defining what discipleship looks like from an individual perspective and for a particular moment in a disciple's life, Matthean churches need to look at their whole community over lifelong journeys. So Matthean faith communities map discipleship on a path that establishes milestones for intentional faith development, passionate worship, risk-taking service, and witnessing. These milestones establish a clear path for inquiring, beginning, intermediate, and mature disciples. To chart these milestones for your context, lay out a table with the realms of discipleship down the left-hand side, and the stages of discipleship across the top.

Once the table has been created, it's time to assess what goes in each of those boxes. Trusted leaders should do that work, because in Matthean churches the trusted leaders can set the direction for the congregation. Mattheans are both good leaders and good followers, but they will only follow those leaders taking beneficial actions for the growth of the community.

For trusted leaders to make beneficial decisions, it is imperative that Matthean churches use strategic thinking to articulate a clear mission and vision. As with Markan churches, the mission need not change, because for Matthean churches the mission can come directly out of the Great Commission: go and make disciples. The vision, however, requires strategic analysis to fit the context in which the church lives and breathes.

When a Matthean church adopts its vision and embraces the strategic thinking behind it, the vision will then significantly shape the discipleship system that the church pulls together. A Matthean church will follow trusted leaders who cast a clear vision and actually take action. As leaders teach the church about their vision, they can focus on the work Jesus needs them to do, which will keep them from working themselves to death by doing things that aren't actually making disciples or fulfilling the mission God has for them.

As the table for the discipleship pathway is filled in, some gaps will be discovered. It will become evident when too many programs are clogging up a particular stage of discipleship. You will also discover that some things the church is doing, perhaps some things dearly loved for a long time, no longer fit into your discipleship strategies. It is time to retire those things. Give them a dignified farewell, but help the congregation understand why they are being discontinued. If those decisions can be framed by a vision the congregation is behind, then the death is less painful. Since new ministries need to launch, it is helpful to put a permission-giving decision path in place that allows action to be taken without too many steps of approval along the way. So simplifying the leadership structures is one way to streamline the decision path. Mattheans prefer a simple and clear structure because unnecessary bureaucracy delays needed action.

Mattheans appreciate clear directions. Like a path cut through a dense forest, Matthean discipleship works out best if it has a clear starting point and ending point (recognizing that discipleship doesn't end in this lifetime). It also works well to have markers along the path to track your progress. As you develop an image that will help convey this system to your congregation, images that mark a journey work particularly well: a path, a road, a map. Use the image to give them a concrete representation of the journey of discipleship, and then use the discipleship table to serve as the to-do list for these disciples. The two in tandem should provide the clarity Mattheans so greatly appreciate.

Steps for Implementing a Matthean Discipleship Pathway

1. Define the mission and vision for your church. Either do this with trusted leaders who are part of existing leadership teams, or form a new vision team.

2. Share the strategic thinking with the congregation. Encourage buy in through regular and persistent communication.

3. Create your table for discipleship milestones. List the stages of discipleship across the top. Along the side list the realms of discipleship.

4. Fill in the boxes on your table (e.g., what would you suggest a beginning disciple do for spiritual growth? An intermediate disciple? A mature disciple?). Make note of any gaps where your church does not offer space for growth, and also note where you have too many offerings. Finally, list all those programs that don't fit anywhere on the discipleship chart.

5. Take the information to whatever boards or teams oversee church programs. Share what you have learned. Teams should then set about to encourage new ministries, and also make plans to retire ones that have outlived their usefulness. This chart will also help you bring elements together to express your Matthean type more fully (e.g., worship and witness).

6. Design a visual element for conveying your discipleship system.

7. Share your discipleship system with the congregation. Regular recourse to it should be shared as part of church gatherings, such as worship. Key leaders should model how they are using it for the congregation as well.
8. Share the discipleship system with newcomers early so that they can begin to integrate their lives and their discipleship in the community. You may want to develop a new disciples class to educate about your mission, vision, and pathways for individual growth.

Hit the Target: Lukan Discipleship

- **Discipleship System:** Relational circles
- **Additional Elements:** Small groups (with built-in disruption or multiplication plans), Fresh Expressions, faith sharing
- **Communicative Image:** Concentric circles/target, web

Lukans love to love. It is the core of who they are. They need a discipleship system that allows them to love more people and love them better. A Lukan journey in discipleship, then, centers around defining and growing in relationships with others.

You may come to the conclusion that you have a Lukan faith community, either from personal observation or because the leadership was tested and they clearly lean Lukan. However, before you proceed with implementing an intentional discipleship pathway based on growing interpersonal relationships, make every effort to test the entire church. Of all the churches, Lukan churches are the ones most likely to resist anything that does not include them in the process. You also can't merely send out an email asking for people to take the assessment. To help people feel included, you need to talk to people individually and ask them to do it.

Explain how important they are to this discipleship process. The personal touch will help the Lukan church know itself better, so we can love each other better.

Once you have established that you are actually a Lukan church and shared what that means with the congregation, by using the model established in the Gospel Discipleship *Participant Guide*, the first thing that a Lukan church needs to do is define its circles of relationships. Then seek to grow those relationships in spiritual practices, participatory worship, risk-taking mission, and shared witness to God's grace in each of those relational circles. Whereas individuals may look at specific relationships (family, church, neighbors), churches may look at the means and social locations for relationships to grow by identifying close, casual, and potential new relationships. For instance, the three circles of relationships for a church might be small groups, the church as a whole, and the wider community. This sort of "geographical" pairing also lines up with the last words of Jesus in Acts (Jerusalem, Judea/Samaria, ends of the earth—the ends of the earth in this case may be the town limits).

Once at least three circles of relationships are established, then it is time to look at what growth in discipleship looks like in each of those circles, while keeping in mind the realms of discipleship. So small groups may center their work around spiritual growth (such as Bible study, prayer, giving, and so on), but they can also integrate worship and service as well. Of course, every small group should be working to grow in numbers, which is indeed the result of witness.

An important principle for establishing a discipleship system in a Lukan community is "intentional disruption." Lukan churches can come to be so protective of the relationships they already have that they sacrifice the potential for new relationships. So Lukans will start small groups with the intention of welcoming new folks in, but then become so insular that no one can break in. Consequently, no place appears for new people to gather in a new circle. As part of their discipleship system, Lukans need to be instructed, encouraged, and cajoled to break their routines. The leaders can set the ground rules for how to do this. Some churches will say when a small group reaches twelve people it needs to break into two. Watch out for Lukans who subconsciously stop inviting people at eleven. Another technique is to empower Mattheans who have been instructed at some point to form a new group, or Markans who will know when it is time based on the Spirit, to start something new regularly. You might put a time limit on groups, meeting together for a year around a particular emphasis, and then the next year shuffling around. Lukans will resist these disruptions. So help Lukans understand that disruption is not to be mean but to make space for new people to love. Leave some groups in place, teach Lukans to lean into their gift of hospitality, but also create new groups with intentional consistency.

Because of their desire to love deeply, which consequently results in Lukans focusing on the people they know, Lukan faith communities struggle with sharing witness with others through evangelism. See the *Participant Guide* for more observation about this challenge. Be sure to include a form of "relational evangelism" in a Lukan discipleship faith community. Examples include "invite a friend to _____" or starting a dinner church. See the literature and websites for the Fresh Expressions movement for additional ideas.[1] Also, equip Lukans on how to talk organically about their faith. The fear of disrupting relationships by talking about Jesus is significant for Lukans, even if it is largely unfounded.

Jesus's last words in Acts give us the image for a Lukan discipleship system, circles. Circles appeal to Lukans because they are inclusive, and because they can also represent union or embrace. If you want to think in terms of the movement from Jerusalem to Judea and Samaria to the ends of the earth, a set of concentric circles like a target readily represents such movement. Place the three circles of relationships in one of each of

1. See Audrey Warren and Kenneth H. Carter Jr., *Fresh Expressions: A New Kind of Methodist Church for People Not in Church* (Nashville: Abingdon Press, 2017) and Michael Beck with Jorge Acevedo, *A Field Guide to Methodist Fresh Expressions* (Nashville: Abingdon Press, 2020).

the circles. Then, you could either make a different set of circles for each spiritual realm, or place the spiritual realms in lines across or surrounding the three circles. This visual helps people conceive of the work of growth that takes place across all aspects of their lives with others.

Steps for Implementing a Lukan Discipleship Pathway:

1. Test the entire church using the Gospel Discipleship assessment. This is to include everyone in the process and increase likelihood of adoption of the system.

2. Be in conversation about the purpose of growth as a disciple of Jesus. Be sure the congregation understands the purpose of intentional discipleship as you share the results of the Gospel Discipleship assessment, preferably with as many people as possible. Remember, Lukan churches need to feel like as many people as possible were included, particularly in whole church efforts.

3. Define your relational circles. Identify at least three (either locations for relationships or people with whom you have or should have a relationship).

4. Discuss and define means of growing in spiritual growth, worship, service, and witness in each of the relational spheres.

5. Communicate your system with the whole congregation.

6. Implement a small group "disruption" process, but make sure people understand the need for such disruption and then make it organic to your context.

7. Provide regular training in hospitality and witness to work your way through typical Lukan discomfort.

8. Create new relational spaces outside of the church with regularity and intentionality. And encourage each person to love one new person every year.

Taking Root: Johannine Discipleship

- **Discipleship System:** Mentor-apprentice pairings
- **Additional Elements:** Congregational nominations, congregational care team, church administrative staff/volunteers, leadership accountability
- **Communicative Image:** Tree, ladder, compass, directional images

A Johannine intentional discipleship system will take patience to unfold. The wait is like planting a seed and allowing that seed to take root and grow. As the roots spread out, though, a bigger plant emerges on the surface, and the whole system becomes incredibly stable, presuming the roots don't get diseased. While slow going at first, in the end it will be incredibly durable, creating a solid foundation of faith on which people may grow.

After a church has taken the Gospel Discipleship assessment and determined it is a Johannine church, it is wise to take stock of its leadership. The leadership will be the trunk from which the whole system flows. Determine whether those who are currently serving in leadership are actually the people the disciples will follow. One way to determine if the leaders can be followed is by surveying the congregation. The survey is short and can simply ask four questions around the realms of discipleship:

1. Who would you go to in our congregation to learn more about spiritual growth and/or scripture?
2. Who would you go to in our congregation to learn more about worship?
3. Who would you go to in our congregation to learn more about service?

4. Who would you go to in our congregation to learn more about witness?

Then tally your results. Those nominated by the congregation are likely your trusted leaders. As you are cultivating a system in which mature disciples mentor growing disciples, you want to start by equipping these people for such work.

Johannine disciples look to the pastor to lead this work in the vast majority of cases. So most Johannine faith communities start out with the pastor working with the church-nominated mentors. Ideally this work would focus in on all four realms of discipleship, acknowledging that everyone will need to grow in at least one of them, and everyone is probably a seasoned pro in at least one of them as well. The pastor will work with this core group of no more than twelve people, regardless of church size. If the church wants to train more leaders in the first phase, an associate pastor can work with a group.

The work of training the trainers will likely take a year. Once that group has been deeply trained in the realms of discipleship, and in mentoring skills as well, that group deploys to mentor their own groups. Those groups can be as small as one-on-one (meetings should occur in public places for healthy boundaries) to groups as large as twelve.

While that initial year of launching a Johannine discipleship system is small, the second year could be exponential, going from twelve people trained by one leader to 144 new folks in mentoring relationships. It is up to your discretion whether the pastor continues to meet with the initial twelve, or if the pastor releases them and works with a new group. If the pastor takes on a new group of twelve, as many as 157 will be in mentoring relationships during the second year.

There are other logistical tactics to put in place as this Johannine system gets off the ground. First, since the pastor is dedicating extra attention to teaching and mentoring, it is a good idea if the pastor has additional support in place to offload some other responsibilities. This would likely include the creation of a congregational care team to help with visits of the homebound and nursing home parishioners, as well as routine pastoral care issues. It also helps to have some administrative support in place, in particular someone who will track involvement in mentoring groups.

The Johannine discipleship system circles back in on itself. Thus the mentor pastor should also have a mentor. The church board or pastor relationship committee should make certain the pastor has a coach or mentor, and the church should hold the pastor accountable for regularly meeting with that person. The pastor also needs good counsel within the congregation, which includes listening to a dissenting voice. The teacher needs a "prophet" who is not afraid to confront when the lead pastor is starting to stray (Markans can often fill this role well; see the section in chapter 2 on a "Markan in a Johannine church"). Because the fall of the central leader is such a significant faith crisis for Johannine churches, such churches need to be intentional about establishing systems of accountability. Don't be afraid to hold the pastor accountable. Failure to do so can allow even the strongest leader to stray, and then the whole system caves in on itself. Rotten roots will kill the tree. And in truth it is usually the stuff buried beneath the surface that creates the rot.

Speaking of trees, when you are helping the congregation learn about and adopt this new system, a tree that grows from a seed can be a compelling metaphor. Other metaphors that work are ladders—climb up toward Jesus as you grow in your discipleship—and compasses, pointing you in the direction you need to journey. The ladder is overtly hierarchical, but that will fit the ethos of some churches, and it does not need to mean that some people are better disciples than others. However, sometimes Johannine faith communities struggle over playing favorites, particularly in who gets to be mentored by the pastor. If you have done congregational nominations, however, you have built the system on congregational favorites as opposed to supposed pastoral ones. Just make sure you communicate that reality as you communicate your new system to the congregation.

Steps for Implementing a Johannine Discipleship Pathway

1. Share the results of the Gospel Discipleship survey with the congregation, and help them understand the value of mentoring relationships in discipleship.

2. Have the congregation nominate people they look to for guidance on spiritual growth, scripture, worship, service, and witness.

3. Pastor meets with up to twelve of the people nominated by the congregation for approximately a year.

4. Put structural vents in place to share the pastoral and administrative load: congregational care team and administrative volunteers or staff.

5. Each of those who were mentored by the pastor takes on their own group to mentor after a year of intense training.

6. Decide if the pastor continues mentoring the same initial group as the core leadership for this system, or if the pastor takes on a new set of apprentices each year. Use earlier nominations to decide on a new group or poll the congregation again.

7. Help people understand that they can set up their own mentoring relationships with people they would like to learn from, building a mentor/apprentice culture, and be sure to explain it to newcomers and integrate them as well.

8. Make sure there is a decision path and people in place to hold the pastor accountable.

Chapter Two

LEAN INTO YOUR TYPE

"Okay, so the predominant pattern is X type in our church. Shouldn't we try to develop discipleship systems for the other three types as well?"

This question, or one like it, is asked frequently. We are accustomed to language that makes everyone welcome, and so we know we need to make a church that has space for everyone. The idea of leaning into one discipleship type makes leaders and participants uneasy. And this question typically comes from someone whose test shows that their spiritual growth does not correlate to the dominant type of their church.

Yet the answer to this question is no.

Leaning into your discipleship type as a church is not the same as saying only these kinds of people are welcome here. In the upcoming section, we will learn how important the nondominant types are to the health of a church. Any church that has only one discipleship type in it will wither and die because there will be no one to challenge the participants to grow in their faith. And nondominant types should also recognize that being part of a church different than their dominant type gives them fertile soil for expressing and growing in their discipleship.

The key reason to avoid spending energy on designing a system that balances all four types is that you would be trying to become a different faith community than the one you are. You will burn out trying.

We recognize that every person is uniquely created, and uniquely reflects the image of God. We also recognize that each church is the body of Christ, but that body is as varied as the individuals who make up the world. Each body of Christ is specially made to reach people in your community. Meanwhile, your church is not the only church in your area. So that means another church down the road or in the next valley is meant to reach people too. God makes us different so that as disciples we can reach different people with the life-changing gospel.

Just as different early Christian communities gave rise to four distinct witnesses in the four Gospels, so we are shaped into distinct Christian communities who resonate with diverse people in our communities. Discipleship is not based on a competition with other faith communities. It is based on cooperation with the grace that is freely available to each of us. As Christian congregations function more and more on the margins of the broader culture, and as the cost of discipleship seems to reduce our numbers in an irreligious society, sometimes we panic and reach for everyone we can. The problem with trying to be all things to all people, which is impossible, is that we risk being nothing to no one.

God has called each congregation to a special mission in a particular place. God gifts your church with a particular group of people who have the capacity to reach particular people in your community. We become "inauthentic" when trying to be something we are not. And ironically we ignore the gifted people God sends our way. You are the Lukan church (or Matthean, or Markan, or Johannine church). Your neighboring Christians are the other ones. Celebrate and cooperate with those who have other gifts and discipleship systems. Then you will reach who you are meant to reach.

A Markan in a Markan Church

Once participants understand what kind of disciple they are, they usually wonder how to live that discipleship out in a particular church. It is potentially easiest to live your discipleship in a church dominated by other people who match your type. As an alternative, consider that you may be a prophetic catalyst in a church that leans into a different type. This may especially be true for Markans, who by their nature push against the dominant view.

Still, if you are Markan, and you find yourself in a Markan church, you might be in a church that has Pentecostal or "Spirit-led" language. This expression can vary from an actual Pentecostal (or charismatic) church to a congregation within any denomination that fosters creative, out-of-the-box forms of ministry. Markan churches will be Spirit-led and Spirit-centered. There will be significant expressions of prayer (though the means of praying will vary widely), and frequently the member of the Trinity most often addressed will be the Holy Spirit.

Markans in a Markan church will typically find their particular gifts valued. It is important for Markan churches to have some mechanism of identifying gifts and then empowering people with those gifts to use them. Such a mechanism may be a formal spiritual gifts test, or it may be the collective ability of the congregation to see and name gifts in each other.

Markan churches are often more experimental than other churches. They do not like to be bound in by expectations. Worship patterns vary widely and often spontaneously, perhaps even week to week. A Markan church stuck in a worship rut can experience pushback from the people. The people may even disrupt worship as a result of inspiration in the Spirit. Markan churches can exhibit those lesser known gifts of the Spirit, like speaking and interpreting tongues.

How do you know if you are in an unhealthy Markan church? When the gift of discernment is absent, and a few select people are orchestrating everything, as if they have spiritual superiority over everyone else. A healthy Markan church recognizes that everyone is gifted and seeks to integrate everyone, as if a new person is the missing piece of the puzzle they are trying to complete for God. Unhealthy Markan churches may have colluding contingents at war with each other, each trying to assert that they know what the Spirit wants better than the others. Challenging or dissenting views are not inherently bad behaviors in Markan churches, since thoughtful dissent sharpens discernment. But if Markan churches who embrace fundamentalism then try to manipulate the Spirit, or try to manipulate others by invoking the Spirit, nothing short of an exorcism will right the ship.

A Markan in a Non-Markan Church

Perhaps, however, you are Markan and you have found yourself drawn to a non-Markan church. Congratulations! The Spirit has called you there to disrupt the system!

Markans in non-Markan churches can have significant influence in such a space. Markans may not feel like they have influence, though, as they often feel like they are the outlier. Like the Markan who chooses to get in elevators and start telling jokes, or the Markan who held up the "no long words" sign in the middle of a pastor's sermons, Markans may seem like the snarky mouths in the congregation. They are probably that. We can't just write Markans off, though, as class clowns or sarcastic loners. Frequently Markans are using humor to deliver a challenge in a way that could be more readily heard than a logical analysis. Non-Markan churches would do well to pay attention to the humor of Markans, to make space for it, and to see if it is pointing the church in a new direction.

Remember that a true Markan is tapped into the desires of the Spirit. That means Markans can see what the church can be. Markans will become increasingly frustrated in churches where little progress is made toward that vision. Markans know, painfully too well, how hard it is to turn a church in the direction of God's vision. They are patient, but only up to a point. A Markan who knows the direction of the Spirit and feels the church is off the path will eventually vent or will leave for another place that may be more open to progress. Markans have a spiritual restlessness. Either the church can continue to evolve and become a new space that will hold a Markan's attention, or a Markan will hop from church to church in search of a place where the Spirit's vision is more fully expressed by experience.

Markans can find great purpose in a church that is different from their dominant type, especially if they are welcomed as an equal at the table. Let's look at how a Markan would do in each type church.

A Markan in a Matthean Church

Markans and Mattheans can make great partners. Why? Because Markans see what needs to be done, and Mattheans can actually implement it. Remember that a Markan's attention is hard to hold. Markans struggle to maintain long-term ministries. Sometimes this distraction is the Spirit directing the church a different direction. Sometimes, however, this attention deficit is due not to the inappropriateness of the ministry but because the Spirit intends Mattheans to do the long-haul work, and instead is calling Markans to imagine either the next thing or the next adjustment to an existing ministry. When Markans *and* Mattheans are in alignment on something, transformation is almost inevitable.

Markans and Mattheans can experience friction around transitions to a new ministry. Mattheans are dogs at the root, and they will see purpose in continuing something far longer than Markans will. Mattheans need and grow attached to mission and vision. Markans tend to a flash in the pan meant for a particular moment in time. Churches with Markans and Mattheans do well to allow both of them the space to share their stories. Give Markans the space to explain why they think the Spirit is moving in another direction. Give Mattheans the space to narrate the transformation they are seeing, and especially to share with Markans the transformation they hope to see and how they plan to get there.

Markans and Mattheans will typically be compatible in how they meet in committees or ministry teams. Both want to do what needs to be done, agree on that quickly, and get moving. Markan-Matthean meetings will typically be shorter than Lukan-Johannine meetings, and Markans or Mattheans can at times chafe in meetings dominated by Lukans or

Johannines. One significant difference in Markans and Mattheans in such spaces, though, is that Mattheans are glad to be in charge of the meetings, and Markans would rather be the voice to the side who either pops in with humor to redirect, or only speaks when they have something significant to say. But when they do speak, they expect that everyone will listen because they are speaking on behalf of the Spirit.

A Markan in a Lukan Church

We start by affirming what these two have in common. Both Markans and Lukans regard people with a high value. Lukans value people because they are people. Markans value people because everyone is gifted by the Holy Spirit to play a part in bringing God's reign to earth. Lukans and Markans typically work hard at making space at the table for everyone, for different reasons.

One test church is a Lukan-Markan church, which was asked where Lukans and Markans experience friction. A daughter who is (secondarily) Markan, sitting next to her Lukan mother, said, "Well, Markans will get irritated with Lukans." This friction is present at times because Lukans don't move fast enough for Markans. Lukans can discuss everything to death, and Markans want to move on to what the Spirit is trying to do. The mother and daughter laughed, and recounted that just the day before the daughter had said, "Why are we talking about this again?"

Markans help Lukans move. Markans will do so, though, sometimes without all the discussion that Lukans think they need. Up to a point, that can be a very good thing. That same test church has a pastor who scored highest among all takers on one discipleship type. He is effectively Markan and nothing else, yet he had a Lukan church on his hands. He knew that straight rows of chairs for worship are frustrating for relational participants. Rather than discussing a new arrangement with his worship team or administrative board, he rearranged the chairs on his own. He bent the space to half of an octagon, and put the altar in the center. Lukans grumble when you don't talk with them about it first, and they won't know where their people are going to sit. Perhaps they would see it is a better arrangement for who they are. As predicted they walked in, complained about it, sat down, and realized they could see all their people and loved it. They were still uneasy because there had been no conversation about it, but glad to see faces they loved.

Ultimately, that is how Lukans and Markans live best together—by making space for one another, which comes from both valuing people. Markans can come to understand that part of a Lukan's gift is in building and maintaining relationships, then understanding that Markans will make space for Lukans to express that gift. Lukans also should remember that Markans will expect available space for them too, and they will move much faster than a Lukan is comfortable moving. By making space for a Markan, Lukan churches become healthier. First, Markans actually see the new people who come in the door, whereas Lukans sometimes become so focused on taking care of the existing people that they don't even see new folks coming in. Markans will take notice, so Markans can help make Lukan churches more welcoming. Also, Markans are especially good at removing the power of a bully, if not the bully themselves, which is something that a Lukan will find very difficult to do. Markans will not tolerate someone abusing God's people and belittling them out of using their gifts. Lukans, set your Markans free to limit power where it needs to be limited, and empower those who need to be empowered. If you do, all your relationships will flourish.

A Markan in a Johannine Church

As an example of limiting power, consider the biblical stories about David, who needed Nathan to hold him accountable. Hezekiah needed Isaiah. Ahab needed Elijah. A Johannine pastor needs a Markan. Markans in Johannine churches are called by the Spirit into the role of prophet, even though a Johannine pastor usually will assume that speaking for God is his or her role instead. Indeed, speaking for God is the pastor's role in the congregation. A Markan's role is to be a prophet, speaking truth to power, to the pastor or the leadership in general.

A Markan's ability to see manipulation of the Spirit means that Markans see spiritual abuse at work faster than other types. A Johannine church should pay careful attention to the words of the Markans among them. Pay attention to whether or not your Johannine leaders include Markans among their trusted relationships. Markans are *not* yes men and women. They are Spirit men and women. This means that no matter how wise and good a Johannine leader is, he or she will eventually run sideways with a Markan. The faith community would do well to watch how that kind of discipleship disagreement unfolds. If the Johannine leader wholly rejects the words of the Markan, or even tries to characterize the Markan as wicked in some way, the community should take serious note. A Markan can be as corrupt as anyone, and can certainly become drunk on perceived power in the Spirit. Yet most Markans understand the consequences of such actions. Markans know ultimately there is no hiding from the conviction of the Spirit. Yet Johannines are particularly susceptible to abuses of power. A Markan can help them keep that in check. Johannines can be extraordinary bullies. A Markan with a support group, who is charismatically empowered by the Spirit, can stop the abuse of toxic faith. Markans will keep power distributed in a more equal or flattened way in a Johannine church. This call to an egalitarian church culture is not easy work. It is important work, though. Where Johannine churches organize in a very hierarchical manner, Markans remind the community that such a hierarchy is only meant to organize mentoring relationships, not to make some people better than others. Markans help Johannines live more fully into the values they actually want to have. A Johannine church that runs off or marginalizes their Markan disciples should be approached cautiously. God may not be present in that space.

A Markan can find great purpose in a non-Markan church. Non-Markan churches need them. But Markans may not be disciples loyal to one church during their entire life. Markans will move where the Spirit moves them. We all need and are blessed by Markans, but we also need to let them go. And Markans need to be ready to go, whenever that time may be. If you are a Markan disciple, God calls you to be a spiritual nomad.

A Matthean in a Matthean Church

Is there anyone who feels greater purpose than a Matthean in a Matthean church? Probably not. There may also not be anyone who is busier. Matthean churches do not lack for things to do, and Mattheans do not lack for enthusiasm to do it. Let's reflect on how that plays out.

Mattheans feel that their faith is most alive when they are acting on what they believe. Matthean churches, then, are typically loaded with activities. Most likely if a Matthean wants to do something for Jesus, a Matthean church has that something. Mattheans in Matthean churches do not lack options, and that in itself may be the problem. If you have a bunch of overachieving volunteers in a church that is happy to create more opportunities to volunteer, you may soon have a bunch of worn-out people, and a church spread too thin to sustain any one thing well. Someone needs to make sure that the ministry tasks tightly fit the mission. Naturally there are plenty of people in Matthean churches who want to be in charge!

Mattheans love a concise, action-driven mission for a church. They will often be energized by a church mission that calls its people to know, grow and go. Or love, learn, and lead. They want action, and they love it when their church organizes around actions. Mattheans will resonate with churches that have vows, particularly solemn promises of action, and they will be happy to live into those promises.

Matthean churches will offer all the tracks needed for well-rounded discipleship (at least as Mattheans understand it). Matthean churches will have participatory worship, with laypeople at work throughout the service, either formally as liturgists and musicians, or informally in the general participation in singing and corporate prayers. Mattheans insist on passing the plate, and they give with a concerted sense of duty and purpose.

Matthean churches probably offer multiple class options, where participants can learn how to put their faith in action. And Mattheans will offer all kinds of ways of serving the community. Mattheans can be very good about working outside their walls. A Matthean in a Matthean church is drawn to the opportunities available for service.

Organized religion is a phrase that accurately captures Mattheans in a Matthean church. Mattheans look for a churchy church, which is why most denominations will have some churches that are firmly Matthean. This is a marriage of the hands and feet of Jesus with the arms to the plow church. Still, this focus on doing can neglect some key aspects of intentional faith development. Thus a Matthean church needs other discipleship types in their church. It is also why other church types need Mattheans—they bring the action to everyone's faith expectations.

A Matthean in a Non-Matthean Church

This chapter of the congregational guide was inspired by two Mattheans who were part of non-Matthean pilot churches. They wanted to know what purpose they had in a non-Matthean church. They wanted to know what they were supposed to do.

It is conceivable that if a church doesn't have some Mattheans, that church would never do anything. Or at least, it would be difficult to sustain ministries. But Mattheans aren't just the "doers." Mixed with the other types, they bring important balance to the others that they all need. Mattheans in non-Matthean churches are validated when coworkers understand how critical their energy and movement are to the mission of the church. In fact, without Mattheans, the church might forget what its mission is or could be. Thankfully, Mattheans partner well with others, especially when everyone is focused on the same goals.

A Matthean in a Markan Church

Mattheans and Markans can be inspired pairs. In the first place, they tend to move so much faster than Lukans and Johannines. Second, Markans can provide the inspiration for an idea and a new direction, and then Mattheans can make it happen. Whereas Markans like to inspire, they don't always like to lead, but there are usually some hard-driving Mattheans who are happy to step up.

Mattheans and Markans also draw from each other's energy. My favorite ministry partnership thus far has been with a Matthean. I would brainstorm these crazy ideas, and then my Matthean friend would say, "Let's do it!" Where I would have the inspiration, she would have the grit and determination to make it happen. We could move with incredible speed, too. Literally two days before Halloween, I came up with the idea to go reverse trick or treating: we knocked on our neighbors' doors and gave them treats instead of taking them. In less than forty-eight hours, we had baked piles of cookies, printed a happy greeting, bagged the cookies, attached the greeting, come up with ridiculous costumes, and knocked on fifty-plus doors in the rain to visit with neighbors we had never met.

Mattheans and Markans can clash when Markans feel it is time to stop doing a ministry. Mattheans are not likely to give up until all possibilities are exhausted. Markans will feel restless about a ministry before Mattheans do. This can cause them both some consternation. They need to make space to discuss why one wants to drop it and the other wants to stay. It may simply be that their partnership on something, rather than the ministry itself, needs to sever. Just as Paul and Barnabas eventually split and went different directions, so a Markan and Matthean may need to go their separate ways. Yet as with the parting of Paul and Barnabas, there is potential to reach that many more people.

A Matthean in a Lukan Church

Some Mattheans might say, "I wouldn't want to be part of a Lukan church." The core struggle between Mattheans and Lukans is the definition of mission. For Mattheans, the (com)mission is the mission. For Lukans, people are the mission. The late Lyle Schaller wrote about the missional differences between "first commandment churches" (Go and make disciples) and "second commandment churches" (Love your neighbors as yourself). These two instructions, in the extreme, suggest a difference between "doing for people" and "being with people." Mattheans and Markans become anxious by how much Lukans want to talk about something before doing something about it. Mattheans like to identify the issue, come up with a way to address it, and then do that. Lukans like to make sure everyone has the space to share their perspective before an action is taken. Sometimes, that means Lukans choose not to take action.

This understanding, when a faith community becomes self-aware about how to live out their discipleship, is why Mattheans are needed in a Lukan church. Lukan churches will stand still without Mattheans. Lukans are so worried about offending anyone or losing anyone, they will not make any changes. Mattheans remind Lukans that Jesus sends us out to do work and serve among the people. Mattheans even remind Lukans that they specifically are called to that—to move from Jerusalem to Judea and Samaria to the ends of the earth. Without Mattheans (and Markans), Lukans will remain cozy in the upper room. Unlike Markans, though, who tend to take action without any discussion, Mattheans will try to work things through the proper systems, through the order of the church. Still, Mattheans can get Lukans to move! Sometimes such movement happens because Mattheans drag the Lukans with them.

A Matthean in a Johannine Church

Mattheans are worker bees who love the strategic thinking that goes into a compelling vision. Johannine pastors are great at leading into a vision and telling people how to get there. Mattheans love good instructions. Johannines know how to instruct.

Mattheans are liable to thrive in a Johannine church. Both Mattheans and Johannines resonate with the idea that Jesus serves as our example of how to live. Johannines are good at spelling that out, and Mattheans are good at taking the teaching of a Johannine and putting it to good use. Mattheans will affirm what Johannines teach, since teaching is in fact one of the elements in the Great Commission.

Mattheans will bristle in a Johannine church, however, if they sense that the focus of the church has become less about the mission and more about the leader. Mattheans, ritually driven as they tend to be, do not like a cult of personality. They are not there to worship an ideal example of someone other than Jesus; they are there to learn how to serve as a good example. Mattheans, then, with their own drive to act and at times to lead, will challenge a Johannine cult. However, if the leader is doing a good job of keeping them busy, they are less likely than a Markan to notice what has happened or is happening if a leader becomes corrupt or toxic.

Mattheans, no matter what their context, keep the church moving. Churches would do well to celebrate the lengths they go to give of their time and energy for serving Jesus. Churches would also do well, however, to remember that they can lose Mattheans over two things: not doing enough to change the lives of people in the communities around them and letting the Mattheans do all the work. Mattheans give out over insignificance or exhaustion. So share the load with Mattheans. They can carry a tremendous amount, but we shouldn't expect them to carry it alone.

A Lukan in a Lukan Church

A Lukan in a Lukan church feels "at home." This is family, whether biological or not. It is enough that they are all the family of Christ. Like family, from time to time Lukans will disagree. But for the most part, they are in it together, and can't imagine doing life without one another.

In fact, Lukans do life together well, and so they look for more shared life experiences. These are the churches who know to show up with food when someone dies. Before that, though, they know to go by the hospital. Or the nursing home. Or at least make sure someone else is going by (often they mistakenly think it has to be the pastor, so they will bug the pastor about going to see the homebound). Lukan churches have great potlucks, and Lukans, even as busy as some of them are with their other relationships, are present in such times of fellowship.

Lukans will also thrive in churches that have leaned into Lukan tendencies and have small group opportunities. Lukans need spaces where they can develop intimate connections with others, and Lukan churches tend to provide just such opportunities. What Lukans and Lukan churches need to remember, however, is that they need to be intentional about making space for new people. Introverts in particular, who can find the intimacy of such close relationships very appealing, may have a hard time breaking into established groups in Lukan churches. Remember that Lukans can become rather cliquish. That can mean not even making space for new Lukans. New Lukans in particular will be hurt by such rejection.

Lukan worship should include opportunities for fellowship. These churches will likely be ones that have sharing of joys and concerns, either within the service or on a printed list. They may also have a passing of the peace. Coffee and donuts outside (or inside) the sanctuary are also signifiers for Lukan churches or the Lukans in any church. Lukans yearn for ways to show hospitality, which allows them to share who they are.

Evangelism is expressed through hospitality in Lukan churches, and Lukans should be encouraged to be steady about it. Lukans share their faith as living examples with people they love and who love them. Giving space to share God moments in worship, or to share faith stories in small groups allows Lukans not only to grow in their own understanding of faith but also helps them build confidence in sharing their lives with others. Lukans may find this easiest to do in a Lukan church where they feel the love and comfort of family.

Lukans in a Lukan church will find a space where love of God and love of each other is highly valued. Lukan churches will be reliable in how worship plays out, and in the rhythm of how things are done. Lukans love to keep doing things the way they have always done things, not out of stubbornness but out of respect for doing the things that keep the community happy and together. Lukans may have a hard time in another kind of church. They will certainly struggle over whether to ever leave a Lukan church once they find one.

Lukans in Non-Lukan Churches

Lukans can be incredible reminders of love in the other types of churches. Their theme song is "They'll know we are Christians by our love." We all need some Lukans like this in our lives. As we look at what Lukans bring to the table, Lukans might actually bring the table!

A Lukan in a Markan Church

As discussed under the "Markan in a Lukan Church" section, Lukans and Markans both put a high value on people, for different reasons. Markans value the gifts people bring to the table; Lukans value the people who come to the table. Lukans help Markans remember to check in with people as decisions are being made so that everyone experiences greater inclusion (though Markans will make some snap decisions, ideally driven by the Holy Spirit, and that will almost always make Lukans uneasy). Both Markans and Lukans want everyone at the table. If they remember that about each other, they can make wonderful partners in ministry.

Lukans are sometimes disturbed by the lack of predictability among Markans. Therefore, Lukans can bring a sense of stability to what might otherwise be an impulsive Markan church. Lukans can also help Markans remember that there is a person who is offering a gift, not just a gift attached to a person. They help Markans live more fully into their own values, taking the whole being into account as Markans empower people. Both Lukans and Markans can appreciate powerfully emotional experiences, some of which are created in the creative and unbound spaces of Markans, and some of which are created when people walk authentically alongside one another through life.

A Lukan in a Matthean Church

Lukans in a Matthean church have the capacity to be transformative for the mission-minded Mattheans. Mattheans can get so caught up in doing mission that they may neglect the relational aspect of service. This means that Matthean churches sometimes become havens for handouts rather than for work that actually transforms the conditions that lead people to need the handouts. Lukans, interested in hearing the stories of people and getting to know people, will make time to learn about the real lives of people. If Lukans bring those stories to Mattheans, they may stop the handouts dead in their tracks, especially if Mattheans learn their ministry is doing more harm than good.

An example of a good Lukan-Matthean partnership is a church that historically hosted an Angel Tree ministry. But they were hearing stories about people returning the gifts, and they were also hearing that some families who really needed assistance with Christmas felt too much shame over receiving a handout. They learned these stories from relationships that people in their congregation had. So, the missions team decided to organize a Christmas store instead, where parents could pay ten dollars for a fifty dollar gift card, and then they shopped at the store, where donated toys and games were marked about one-third off what they would cost in the store. Further, some in the church saw an opportunity to get to know their neighbors better and proposed that hosts would walk around with each parent to help them find what they were looking for and to hear the parents talk about their children and their lives. It was an enormous undertaking, but with the influence of both disciples who insisted on doing something to meet the needs of their neighbors (the Mattheans) and disciples who wanted to walk alongside parents to get to know them and to preserve their dignity (the Lukans), the ministry reached more people and made more meaningful connections, some of which resulted in those same parents attending and serving in the church. Lukan-Matthean partnerships connect the actions of faith to the practice of love.

A Lukan in a Johannine Church

Lukans and Johannines share an appreciation of a close relationship. Both of them appreciate one-on-one relationships, though they may serve different purposes, and they may have different power dynamics. Lukans may have more of a drive to equalize friendships and partnerships, while Johannines seek more of a teacher-student dynamic. Still, because Johannines tend to serve both as a mentor and a mentee, these distinct power dynamics may not be plainly evident, and so Lukans may feel very at home in such a structure. Lukans will also appreciate the fact that the pastor tends to stay for longer tenure in Johannine churches than in others.

Lukans are good for Johannines, however, because of the insistence on including everyone. Both Johannines and Lukans can be cliquish, but again for different reasons. Johannines may look as though they have cliques because of the way their discipleship spreads out. In Johannine churches, the pastor mentors a few key leaders, who are then called to mentor the next set of leaders, who are then called to mentor the next set, and so on. That method requires steady attention to maintain growth. Otherwise, a few get mentored, and the rest are treated as students who are not yet ready to advance in their discipleship. Lukans want everyone included in the family, and so they seem to be insistent about their need to be mentored as well as others. Lukans keep Johannines attentive to their values by reminding them that people actually allow them to live those values out. Without relationship, there is no mentoring.

Lukans may push against Johannine culture if they feel too much like the leaders are dictating what is supposed to happen. Remember that Lukans like to have conversations before decisions are made. In some cases, the conversations are the point. If Lukans too often encounter a leader who comes in and announces what is going to happen, Lukans will start to push back. It may be a gentle resistance, but Johannines would do well to pay attention, because if Lukans are pushing back, they have likely wanted to do so for a lot longer you think.

Lukans are the people of love who love the people. Lukans will help us all remember the Greatest Commandment, that we are to love God with all our heart, mind, soul, and strength, and we are to love our neighbor as ourselves. Lukans keep the heart of who we are beating and living in our midst.

A Johannine in a Johannine Church

How fulfilling it is to sit in worship facing the pulpit, listening to a great preacher expound on the Bible, going deep to give us instruction for our lives today! A Johannine in a Johannine church will think this way on a regular basis. Johannine disciples love to learn from great teachers. Johannine churches put great teachers at the head of the church. A weak teacher or preacher will not survive long in a Johannine congregation. In the first place, there will be plenty of people in the pews who have studied well. They expect to learn from their preacher, and if they don't, they will work to get someone else. In the second place, great preachers and teachers will be most appreciated by a Johannine congregation, so why would they ever leave?

Because Johannine congregations tend to hold on to their pastors for a significant length of time (if they can make it past the two-year mark), Johannine disciples tend to enjoy being in a Johannine church because they can settle into learning from their pastor over the long haul. Most Johannine disciples are drawn to congregational churches (churches that hire their own pastor) rather than connectional churches (churches that are sent a pastor by a bishop or other ecclesial authority). An exception would be a very large church in a connectional system, since very large churches lean toward congregationalism and tend to keep their pastors for a longer length of time. This is helpful for Johannine disciples who long to be shaped and mentored by a central leader. A Johannine can also thrive in a church that has other significant leaders too, if the church is either between pastors or is so large that access to the senior pastor is mainly in worship.

In most Johannine churches, worship will be the central organizing element of church life. Even in smaller churches, the bulk of learning and mentoring will probably happen in the sanctuary. However, because Johannines seek mentoring and teaching and tend to become mentors and teachers, the other strength of a Johannine church is its classes and small groups. Each of these groups will probably also be led by someone well respected with significant teaching skills.

Scripture will be central to Johannine churches, and Johannine disciples should find in such a church plenty of opportunity to study the Bible. Again, this may be through classes and small groups, or it may take place primarily in worship. Johannines will not be surprised, or upset, that the sermon takes up half of the worship service. With that expectation, they don't want their time wasted, and weak preaching will not last in such churches.

As Johannine disciples mature in their faith, they will expect to take central roles of leadership, either on committees or as teachers and mentors themselves. Johannine churches will never lack for people ready to lead. They may need discernment about who should lead at what time. Also, because Johannines have such a high bar when it comes to expectations around teaching, some of the disciples in the congregation, who could lead and teach well, may be too intimidated to come forward. Johannine disciples should be encouraged to grow in their discipleship by making such steps, and others who have led for a long time should be prepared to step to the side and mentor the next generation to come forward.

A Johannine in a Non-Johannine Church

Like the other disciple types, Johannines will be most comfortable in a church type that matches them. However, Johannines have great gifts to offer the Markan, Matthean, and Lukan churches, but Johannines are liable to struggle in non-Johannine churches. This struggle may be due to theological differences: most Johannines lean to the more theologically and socially conservative tribes in Christianity. These churches still avoid accepting women as preachers and often are organized by a clearly defined hierarchical structure. Churches that share leadership in a more horizontal rather than vertical way may not fit with a Johannine desire for learned mentors teaching new apprentices.

Still, Johannines bring great gifts to non-Johannine churches. Chief among these gifts is a deep appreciation for (and often significant skills at) teaching. Johannines also bring with them an appreciation of wisdom, and that can be significant in fostering intergenerational exchange. Depending on which type church they are in, however, those strengths can manifest in very unique ways.

A Johannine in a Markan Church

Johannines and Markans share one key sensibility: a deep appreciation of giftedness. The distinction between them is that Markans believe everyone is gifted, and Johannines believe that those gifts need to be nurtured to reach their full potential. A Johannine in a Markan church, then, can be a key person in developing gifts, particularly in those disciples who lack confidence in their gifts. Where a Markan may just assume that anyone who knows they have gifts also knows how to develop them (or assumes the Holy Spirit has gifted them either with what they need or the knowledge of how to get it), Johannines take a step back and take the time to work with someone to plan their development.

Johannines, then, are good people to put in an advisory capacity in Markan churches. Markans should put a means in place to identify the gifts of people who come into their church. Johannines, who are typically gifted in and value mentoring, could readily serve in the counseling capacity in that system. For instance, the Markan go-to for identifying gifts is to offer a spiritual gifts test. Johannines could then sit with someone and go over their results, helping that person plan how they will develop and offer those gifts in the community. Johannines have the patience for this work, where Markans may not.

Johannines and Markans will most likely clash in their understandings about the distribution of power. Where Johannines are comfortable with top-down hierarchies, Markans will want power spread out across the community. Johannines, then, are liable to grow frustrated with the absence of a strong central teacher in a Markan church. They may also bristle at what they could perceive as chaos in the worship service. Johannines prefer a sermon-centric service, and Markans may emphasize other moments in the service, such as prayer. Or the sermon may be a creative element such as a dramatic reading or an interpretation of art. Johannines would much prefer a straight teaching sermon on the scriptures. Markan worship, then, may be a frustration for a Johannine, depending on how deeply a Markan church has leaned into its unbound Holy Spirit identity.

A Johannine in a Matthean Church

Johannines and Mattheans are the drivers of discipleship. They appreciate that about each other. If you want something done, and want it done efficiently and with well-defined leadership and goals, look for a Johannine-Matthean pair. One of the pastors tested as Johannine-Matthean, and he is the most likely candidate to be a megachurch pastor. He is constantly moving and doing, and he is usually in charge of all the things he is doing. Johannine-Mattheans get things done. Period.

Johannines can help Mattheans remain focused. Remember that a struggle of Mattheans is that they get tempted to do everything that comes their way. Johannines can be very useful to Mattheans because Johannines can be good at narrowing the focus. These are the people who can tightly define a mission and vision, and then lead Mattheans into that reality. Johannines can keep Mattheans from being busy just for busyness sake. Johannines remind Mattheans what their purpose is for the things they do.

Mattheans and Johannines also both appreciate good teaching. Johannines are frequently good teachers, or at least care enough about it that if they find themselves teaching they will work to do it well. Mattheans will really appreciate that about Johannines.

One frustration likely for this pair is having too many cooks in the kitchen. Because Mattheans and Johannines can both be strong leaders, or at least both have a tendency to want to be in charge, there may be significant friction between them. Add to the mix that Johannines really have high expectations of their leadership, particularly for their leaders to be strong moral examples, where Mattheans want their leaders to be doing things all the time. The difference in expectations may frustrate both of them (not to mention exhaust their leader). They should learn to share leadership and to make room for each other's strengths and weaknesses.

A Johannine in a Lukan Church

Lukans and Johannines value close relationships. The distinction is in the purpose of the relationships. Lukans seek friends. Johannines seek mentors or mentees, depending on what role the Johannine is playing. This means that Lukans and Johannines can become very close. They should, however, have a conversation between them about what each expects from the purpose of the relationship. You can be in a friendship, and you can be in a mentorship, but it is very difficult for those two things to exist together. A mentor-apprentice relationship necessarily maintains some distance so the mentor can maintain some level of objective observation to offer constructive direction. Friends should be on even footing regularly, with either person periodically playing the role of offering advice or guidance. In a friendship that role is interchangeable. In a mentorship, it is not. To avoid misunderstanding, it is wise to have clarity about the purpose of a relationship between a Lukan and a Johannine.

Johannines have a greater drive than Lukans to connect with new people. Lukans are hospitable and welcoming, but they also get very attached to the people they know. Johannines can help Lukans continue to see more people, and to seek more people. Johannines will seek new people to share the knowledge of Jesus Christ with them; their teaching drive helps make them active evangelists. They want to mentor the world into faith in Christ, at least once they feel confident enough in their own faith to do so. Johannines can help push Lukans out of their box to meet new folks, as much as Lukans may initially resist that. However, Lukans are likely to be unnerved by a Johannine's willingness to talk about Jesus with someone before a deep relationship is established. Lukans may see Johannines as pushy.

Indeed, Johannines often are the bullies in a Lukan church. With some exceptions, Johannines don't set out to be the bullies in a Lukan church. Instead these high expectations that Johannines have—and God knows we could all do with some healthy higher expectations than most churches have—become points of contention for them in the church. They are pushing to get Lukans to teach more about the faith and preach more about the Bible, and they start to fill a role of pushing against people. Johannines may experience quite a bit of success at getting what they want in a Lukan church too, because Lukans like to please people, and often they will let someone have what they want, especially if that person feels strongly about it. Somewhere along the way, the power that Johannines experience corrupts them. They lose sight of the value of the people around them, and instead become dogmatic about the beliefs that they personally hold. While their motivations may have initially been good ones, as unhealthy patterns have developed, they have fallen into a corrupt pattern of seeking to impose their righteousness on others. Ironically, if a Johannine becomes self-aware of this need for control, he would be deeply grieved about it. Unfortunately, usually by that point, a Johannine is so committed to seeing beliefs and convictions put into practice that she can't see the moral harm she is doing to others. It will either take a coached and committed team of Lukans, a Markan who is convicted to throw out that prideful evil, a Matthean who has been instructed to limit a Johannine's power, or perhaps another Johannine (though we may be trading one bully for another), to constrain a Johannine bully's power. The Johannine actually may need to leave the church and will probably be better off going to a Johannine church where the big fish can be a minnow in a big lake of other Johannines. This will be painful for Lukans, who hate to see anyone go, but we all need to realize that in some cases, for the health of the church and for the soul of a Johannine who has unintentionally become a bully, a change may be exactly what is needed, and may also reflect God's will.

Johannines can be strong personalities, and that is driven from a deep love of learning about God. They also tend to have well-defined moral compasses. At times our churches stray from both teaching and laying claim to moral truths. Johannines help us all keep those convictions before us. We can be thankful for their commitment to the belief that Jesus is in fact the way, the truth, and the life.

Chapter Three

STRENGTHS OF EACH TYPE

The Gospel Discipleship process begins with the assumption that all churches are gifted. We also assume that all churches have a purpose that they can live out for Christ in the very place and time in which they find themselves. If the Spirit is still present with them, then there is still life for them to share. In this chapter we lift up the typical strengths of congregations who exhibit each type. Remember, if your church has more than one type with significant numbers in your score, you are likely to have a blend of the strengths of multiple Gospel types. It also likely means that not all the strengths will accurately describe your church, so focus time in reflection about which ones do.

After describing a primary and a secondary strength, one or two options are proposed for expressions of church for each type. In this post-Christendom era (meaning that the church is not in charge of the culture), each church should make some adjustments—or face certain death. So let's be intentional about the adjustments we make, meaning they should make sense for who we are and who we are called to be. If we try to be something we are not, or do not have the capacity to be, we will continue to spin our wheels.

Markan Strengths

Primary Strength: Integrating Everyone (Especially SBNRs)

One strength of a self-aware Markan church is that it can readily integrate anyone who comes in its doors. This ability is not simply due to the expectation that every single person will be tested and counseled and then placed where he or she would best serve. It is likely because Markans truly understand that everyone is gifted by God to have some special purpose, and they are ready to invite that purpose in, to become part of the vision they are living for the Spirit. Markans are set up to adjust the vision as new people come in and change the giftedness of their community.

Another significant aspect of the Markan ability to integrate everyone is that Markans can organically reach out to one of the fastest growing demographics in North America (as well as Europe): people who identify as Spiritual but Not Religious (SBNR). Markans don't reach this population (which has no shape or form) through a spiritual gifts test or any other religious product. They reach SBNRs through their worship. This phenomenon through experiential (often Pentecostal) worship practices has evolved and spread, often through revival, for one hundred years. These worship services, if still vital, have unpredictability or spontaneity because they create space for the Spirit to show up. Since they expect that the Spirit will show up, the result is that the Spirit does show up in tangible ways that people can actually experience. SBNRs seemingly long for contact with the Holy. Markan churches are the places actually channeling such experiences. Markans reach SBNRs because they are leaning into their Markan identity, a core identity for a faith community that might also be labeled as Spiritual but Not Religious.

Secondary Strength: Innovation

Markans are the creatives of the Christian community. They are also the ones who believe in and have experienced miracles in the present day.

As a result, Markans don't typically see boundaries to what God and God's people can accomplish. They can think differently, and when they put agile structures in place, they can also act quickly. If they have aligned people's gifts with the ways they should serve, they can mobilize in useful and meaningful ways rapidly as well. Markans, in short, are ready to do something new—pretty much all the time.

Markans will sometimes fail at the things they try. Just because Markans get a directive from the Holy Spirit doesn't mean we will manage to pull it off perfectly. However, Markans also understand the risk to experimentation. They also tend to understand that even in failure there is learning, and that makes them better prepared for the next thing. Life with the Spirit is messy. Sometimes it is clumsy. It is exciting but also awkward. Still, for Markans there is nothing else like getting to work with the Spirit. The reward is definitely worth the risk.

Twenty-First-Century Church Expressions for Markans: Experiential, Community Laboratories[1]

Experiential churches show people how to experience God by bringing the Holy explicitly into the everyday. There are many ways of doing that, from Spirit-centered worship services to Messy Church. Markan churches operate in these creative and unbound spaces. Because of their bent toward innovation, Markan churches can envision themselves as community laboratories. One side effect from the separation of church and state is that the church can actually be far more agile than many of our government and corporate entities who are bound by red tape and bureaucracy. The only red tape and bureaucracy that a church has is that which has been self-imposed. Invite your bound-up community into an unbound space in the church, and see what miracles break out.

1. Many of the twenty-first-century church expressions listed here either come from or were inspired by the work by Paul Nixon and Beth Ann Estock, *Weird Church: Welcome to the Twenty-First Century* (Cleveland, OH: Pilgrim Press, 2016).

Matthean Strengths

Primary Strength: Action!

Mattheans are not ones to sit idly by. Idle is not in their vocabulary, except to describe the other faith community types. Mattheans don't like to sit still in their faith. Faith without works is dead. If Mattheans see a need, they will respond to it. In fact, Mattheans will go find a need to respond to before it ever has a chance to come to their door.

If Mattheans have simplified or flattened their church governance, they can be especially quick at response. Mattheans sometimes need to reflect on their efforts before, during, and after, then build plans based on any lessons they have learned for whatever is coming next. Mattheans also can do long-haul ministries and do them well, but they need to see signs of progress all along the way. Mattheans don't like wasting time, energy, or resources, so they need to know the work they are doing is actually doing the good they intend.

Secondary Strength: They Do Church Well

Mattheans know how to do church. You can tell a Matthean church by the breadth of its programs, its institutional strength, the activity of the people. This trait could also be listed under Matthean challenges, because the programmatic, attractional model of church is cyclical. Program churches were strong after World War II and again in the 1970s and into the 1980s, and then seemed to absorb too much energy and cost as the demand became saturated. The programs and their consultants lapsed until the pendulum swung back in the mid-2000s. But now the programs are saturated again amid predictions about the death of the busy "can do" attractional church. Some might even think the Matthean faith communities are about to be extinct.

Let's not forget that we are describing Matthean faith communities who are shaped by a Gospel, with particular good news from God. That

Gospel isn't going anywhere, and neither is that good news. Of course there have always been Mattheans! Of course there will always be Mattheans! They aren't going anywhere. Yet, as the world turns, they need a new definition of how to do church, and then Mattheans will tear it up! Of all the types, Mattheans are probably the most willing to make the moves that need to happen to reach people for Jesus in the twenty-first century, but only when they understand that their core theology of church is not changing. Mattheans benefit from spending time studying and naming their own theology of church. Once they have clarity about what actually constitutes church, they can make the changes they need. Skip this step, though, and Mattheans will become dogmatic about defending everything from the order of worship to the programs church provides. What could be a strength of theirs—understanding the purpose of church—becomes a weakness if they don't do the necessary reflective work.

It might look like a Herculean task to get Mattheans to walk away from how their generation has "always" been doing church. Mattheans can be taught. They should be shown why a different way of doing church is needed. Once they understand that information, though, Mattheans will go. Once Mattheans are on board with a new paradigm, they will do it very well. And if the attractional model of church is waning in favor of a missional model of church, Mattheans know how to organize right into the mission field.

Twenty-First-Century Church Expressions for Mattheans: Mission Outposts, Whatever Works

Since Mattheans are people of action, they do well in a church that is taking action. Mattheans fit well with the concept of a mission outpost church, or a church that is spread throughout its community, with each outpost dedicated to a particular goal of the mission. If you teach Mattheans how to do church in a different way, and they desire to put that learning to use, then you can virtually teach Mattheans to live into practically any strategic vision of church.

Lukan Strengths

Primary Strength: Love

All discipleship types at their best know how to love. Lukans are centered around it. They also practice it with greater ease. Love isn't easy for any of us, especially the kind of love Jesus calls us to, but Lukans are intentional about trying. These are the churches who value their people not for the gifts they bring but for the people they are. Or for the very fact that they are people, plain and simple.

Lukans *try* to love God and neighbor and self. Sometimes the Lukan conception of neighbor becomes very insular, but when they can keep their hearts open and keep seeking to love more and more people, they can become not only the best at fulfilling the Greatest Commandment, they can also become the world's best witnesses, because they build genuine relationships with people and then integrate faith into that relationship. People who feel like they are truly loved and known are far more likely to stay in a church than those who are filling a role. The hiccup for Lukans (and this will come up under challenges) is to keep making room in their hearts to love more people and not just the ones they already know.

Secondary Strength: Staying Power

One of the things that Lukans struggle with is trying anything new—because new things mean someone could get upset, and then they might leave. Lukans hate to lose anyone! Ironically, Lukans are the least likely ones to leave. Markans will leave if they feel a place has lost the Spirit or is ignoring the Spirit. Mattheans will leave if a church isn't doing anything. Johannines will leave if they don't respect the leadership. Lukans, though, just keep staying. In one of the pilot churches for Gospel Discipleship, a Sunday school class was filled with Johannines plus one Lukan. The Johannines became frustrated with the perceived stance of the denomination, and they all left. Despite the fact that an end to a Lukan's small group is a significant faith crisis, she stayed. Lukans stay.

In a world where so much changes all around us all the time, when you can unfriend someone with just the click of a button, there is something admirable about Lukan loyalty and commitment. Pastors should take note if they start seeing loss of Lukans. That is a significant red flag. Find out what is going on to make that happen, because it is rare. Lukans stay.

Twenty-First-Century Church Expressions for Lukans: House Churches, Fresh Expressions

Of course we would throw back to the first century for our stalwart Lukans! Return to the way Christianity spread before when it was not in favor with the culture at large: meet in small groups in houses. Bringing people into our homes is a highly relational, personal space. Lukans will thrive at this kind of church, and again, this has real staying power because people become intimately connected to each other's stories. The Fresh Expressions movement is built around the same concepts, though it is meeting relational needs in more public spaces, such as at McDonald's or a dog park or a tattoo parlor.[2] These groups meet around common affinities and then introduce faith practices gradually, much like the seventy-two were instructed to do when they were sent out from Jesus.

Johannine Strengths

Primary Strengths: Teaching and Learning

Johannine disciples are lifelong learners. That doesn't necessarily translate to strong teaching ability, but people who are passionate about

2. See Audrey Warren and Kenneth H. Carter Jr., *Fresh Expressions: A New Kind of Methodist Church for People Not in Church* (Nashville: Abingdon Press, 2017) and Michael Beck with Jorge Acevedo, *A Field Guide to Methodist Fresh Expressions* (Nashville: Abingdon Press, 2020).

learning do typically make the best teachers. Add to that the fact that Johannines tend to have a passion for the Bible, and you get the one-two punch for Christian education.

A Johannine church, then, should lean into its teaching. It makes sense in a Johannine church for the sermon to take at least half of the worship time. Spending significant time teaching about the Bible will meet the discipleship needs of the people of the church. Johannine churches should also offer a variety of other classes for people to take. Of course these include Bible-based Sunday school classes, but also examine what other fields of expertise your people bring to the table that could be offered to the community at large. Consider offering various life skills classes. Also, Johannine churches should think about partnering with schools in the area. Johannines will be passionate about supporting learning in their community. It is worth noting that the few youth in the pilot church phase who took this assessment have nearly all shown Johannine as a primary or secondary type. This preference may be a dominant experience for youth who are in school, or because youth are seeking guidance for their future. Many youth are longing for a mentoring experience (whether they can articulate that or not). Johannine churches, then, can be very effective in reaching and nurturing the faith of youth.

Secondary Strengths: Standards

Some people love flexibility and gray, liminal spaces that lack definition. Those people are called Markans. For the other side of the coin, look for the Johannines. Before we stereotype Johannines as rigid and unbending (though some are), let's acknowledge that Johannines provide some stability in a rapidly changing world. How? Because any changes they make are first weighed deeply and studied well. They do not move with the fashion but hold to tradition until there is a very compelling reason to change. This stability is appealing to many people. It provides them a reliable comfort. It feels, on some level, as if temporal things are suddenly tied to the eternal.

A high value on tradition paired with a deep respect for learning means that Johannines will also expect solid teaching from their leadership. They will also expect the leaders to exemplify their teaching, which means that Johannines have an interest in accountability. Walk the walk—don't just talk the talk. Johannines have little tolerance for leadership that does not meet high expectations. Such leadership should not expect to last long in Johannine churches.

Twenty-First-Century Church Expressions for Johannines: Mini-seminaries, Young Life

People are starving to death for the wisdom that can be found in the Bible. Johannine churches are primed to share their deep knowledge of the Bible with a desperate world. Johannines need to make a couple of adjustments. The old way of the expert standing up front lecturing to a herd of willing students is practically dead in a media-saturated world. Education in our schools does not work that way anymore. Educators are far more interactive and far more technologically savvy. If Johannine churches want to meet people where they are and offer deep instruction on the Bible and faith, then they need to get up to speed with technology. They also need to make their learning spaces more interactive, including the sermon. To reach millennials and Gen Z, Johannine churches strain to level out the hierarchical nature of their typical structure. Millennials and Gen Z are not going to wait for an invitation to the master's table. Since Johannines are actually well-placed to reach youth, they do well to learn deeply about Gen Z especially. They can do this by working cooperatively with organizations such as Young Life or an equivalent.

Johnnie-Preferred Church Programs for Johnnies:
[illegible]

Chapter Four

CHALLENGES OF EACH TYPE

Just as all churches have strengths that flow from their Gospel Discipleship type, they also face predictable challenges as a result of their type. Just like with the strengths, if you have multiple types, you potentially also face multiple challenges. This section will not only help you identify where your most likely challenges are, it will make recommendations about how to overcome them.

Markan Challenges

Primary Challenge: Will the Real Holy Spirit Please Stand Up?

Ugh. Discerning the Spirit. You want to talk about slippery work. How do you know when the Spirit is really speaking to you? There are those rare moments of crystal clarity when you absolutely know you are standing in the will of God. All too often, though, there are just hints. Remember when Elijah fled from Jezebel and found himself awaiting God in a cave? God did not come in the earthquake, the great wind, or the fire. God came in the stillness, in the silence. The other discipleship types won't find that helpful.

Add to that reality that some people are just misguided. They think they have a word from the Spirit, but it is really just a word from their own desires. Then there are the more insidious people who will actually try to manipulate Markan congregations by claiming to have a word from the Spirit. Someone who tries to buy or coerce the Spirit puts the whole community at risk and faces a potential tragic outcome (see the story of Simon Magus, Acts 8:9-24). It is critical, then, that Markan communities seek ways of checking the validity of Holy Spirit claims.

Primary Challenge Remedy: Space for Discernment

A Markan congregation as it lives into its identity is to immediately offer a spiritual gifts test (in addition to the Gospel Discipleship test, which determines that they are Markan). One gift that test will identify is discernment. Pay attention to who scores high in discernment. Those people should serve in the permission-giving roles of authorizing the work that people feel called to do. To be fair, they should not be alone. Some congregations are predisposed toward the spectacular gifts of the Spirit (such as persons with the gift of healing or those who can speak or interpret tongues). But those who can discern are priceless to a Markan congregation.

Markan congregations should be praying congregations. Everyone. There should be significant space for prayer in worship, in classes, in meetings, in small groups, practically anywhere that Markans gather. It is also assumed that individuals in such a congregation regularly pray. So Markan congregations should be intentional about teaching people about prayer. People should understand there are all kinds of ways to pray: centering, corporate, using objects like beads or icons, active prayer walking, etc. Markans also especially need to be trained in prayer as a listening rather than a petitioning experience. Markan congregations need to practice prayer regularly. That will not only help more people hear the Holy Spirit, it will allow for corporate consensus about the movement of the Spirit.

A Markan pastor shared a tool for discernment she was given years before, when she first began to feel nudges into the ministry. She was trying to decide if she was hearing the voice of God or not. She went to her pastor to ask for help. The pastor pointed her to Philippians 4:8, and said if it fits these criteria, then it is likely from God: "From now on, brothers and sisters, if anything is excellent and if anything is admirable, focus your thoughts on these things: all that is true, all that is holy, all that is just, all that is pure, all that is lovely, and all that is worthy of praise."

Secondary Challenge: You Are Going to Fail

Even if you put all the mechanisms in place to discern the will of the Spirit, even if you designate intentional and regular times for prayer, there will be times when you get something wrong. Or at least you think you do. You may have truly felt the Spirit was in something, and yet it did not turn out like you expected or it did not deliver the results you hoped for. Markan endeavors sometimes feel incredibly disappointing.

Such is the life of experimental ministry. One of the thrilling things for Markan churches is that they get to do things that no one else is trying. That means, all too often, that there is no road map for doing them. They are making the map up as they go along, much like Lewis and Clark did as they mapped the way to the Pacific Ocean. And like the Lewis and Clark expedition, sometimes there are mountains looming before us, mountains that are very clearly evident, and yet we are still fooling ourselves into thinking they will magically part and let us through. Nope. The mountains don't move, no matter how fervent and faithful we are.

Secondary Challenge Remedy: Get Used to Disappointment

In the movie *The Princess Bride*, an epic sword fight ensues between the Man in Black and Inigo Montoya. As Inigo realizes how extraordinary this masked man is, he begs the man to tell him who he really is. "I must know," he says. The Man in Black responds, "Get used to disappointment." Then Inigo, who just moments ago was desperate to have his curiosity quenched, shrugs and goes back to the fight.

That's what fruitful Markan congregations learn to do: shrug and get back in the fight. Failure doesn't feel good to anyone, but if we let it stop us, then how can we call ourselves a people of hope? Of course, that is the real truth of who we are, and it speaks to the value of failure. We stand on the hope of resurrection. We have seen God take the world's most significant failure—death, particularly the death of the world's Savior—and turn it into the world's greatest success, the resurrection.

Markan communities should learn to look at everything they do with resurrection eyes. When it looks like something they have done is a flop, look at it from a different angle and see what life and learning came out of it. Sometimes that involves taking the long view. For this reason, fruitful Markan churches carve out time for reflection on all the things they do. Whether a ministry is a success or not, stop to evaluate what happened, and to share multiple perspectives on what happened (remember how Pentecost occurred among people with different perspectives) so that lessons are learned. It may also be, however, that you see that your definition of success was off. Frequently we look at things with the world's eyes and not God's. The Holy Spirit so often was up to something we never saw coming. It is also true that the Holy Spirit works within our mess, so even if we do screw something up, the Spirit redeems it anyway.

Lewis and Clark did make it to the Pacific Ocean. They had to ditch their canoes and learn to climb mountains, but when they stood on the Oregon shores, they could look back and see what a remarkable journey they had been on. So shrug it off, and get back on the path.

Matthean Challenges

Primary Challenge: Exhaustion

Mattheans are very excited about doing things. So excited that often they will do things just to be doing things. Matthean churches, then, have a tendency to become program heavy. This may especially be the case if they institute a new program, and then just never let it go, even if it has outlived its usefulness. Matthean-Lukan churches in particular will face a challenge with the inability to shut something down because no one wants to hurt the feelings of the person who started it. Matthean churches, then, can become vastly overextended, and they may significantly waste resources (human and material) just to keep doing things.

Primary Challenge Remedy: A Clear Mission and Vision

Matthean churches need a clear mission and vision in place, and then everything they do should be evaluated according to whether that fits their mission and vision. Sometimes a Matthean or Johannine pastor can lead this process, but if not, then a layperson or team of lay people should be assembled. Once you have clarity about goals, you will know what you need to do to reach those goals. Or at the very least you can ask whether the things you do are on the path. Then become ruthless in saying goodbye to anything that does not further the mission. Encourage everyone to stand behind and see the vision, and to get involved in a reasonable scope of activity that works toward that vision.

While working with churches to test the validity of this Gospel Discipleship framework, people completed the test and then a couple of volunteers came forward to answer three questions to illustrate that they would always answer these three questions in ways that reflected their discipleship type. These three questions get to the heart of the vision and mission of a church. Though there are many helpful resources with strategic thinking to guide development of a mission and vision, for a quick glimpse ask as many people in your congregation as possible to answer these three questions, and then test your mission and vision from the responses you receive. Don't forget that a mission is not only about the people presently within the congregation but also the people nearby whom you are called to reach.

1. When did you (or have you) most felt like a disciple of Jesus?

2. You are in an elevator with ten floors to go, and someone asks you to tell them about your church. What do you tell them?

3. You are in line at the grocery store, and you hear the person behind you say that she would just like someone to tell her about Jesus. You are convicted to turn around. In the time you have before you have checked out, what do you tell her?

Secondary Challenge: Dividing the Haves from the Have Nots (or the Dos from the Do Nots)

Mattheans like fast results. They like to see that the actions they take have an immediate effect in the lives of people. This can be especially true of Matthean-Markans, who like to act quickly and move on to the next thing. In other words, Mattheans sometimes prefer to do "Band-Aid ministry." Someone is hurting, so stop the bleeding. They are quick to respond to immediate needs. What they tend not to do, though, is to address the root cause. They don't take time to ask how the person got injured in the first place. Their focus tends to be on mercy rather than justice.

Responding to immediate needs has value. People get in a ditch sometimes and they need someone to pull them out. The problem recurs if we keep returning to the ditch and getting the same people out. Not only does that drain everyone's energy and resources, it doesn't meaningfully transform anyone. It even erects a divide between the people who are helping and those who are being helped. That kind of relationship can never become one among equals. The people receiving the charity tend to feel less than the ones who are helping, and the ones who are helping start to resent the ones they are helping, viewing them as lazy and as people (or less than humans) who have no purpose for even existing. If someone can't do something, what good is that person?

Secondary Challenge Remedy: Get Down in the Ditch for the Long Haul

Mattheans should learn to take a long view of addressing some of the realities in their community. By learning to walk alongside people, they stop moving and listen to the stories of the people around them. They understand that when we are building the reign of God, it's not enough to spackle the cracks in the walls or caulk the windows. Since Mattheans love systems, some can work out why the foundation is causing the cracks in the first place.

Some action-focused Mattheans get frustrated because they don't see quick and dramatic results. So Matthean faith communities can help the activists to see the big picture. First, make sure that the long-haul work is thoroughly aligned with your mission and vision, because it takes a purpose to sustain this work. Second, take time to celebrate the small victories. As you walk alongside people, you will hear the victory stories. You will also experience transformation yourself. Those stories must be heard to keep encouraging people in their work. And third, you still need to keep doing some of the short-term, Band-Aid responses, while making sure that those works do not interfere with the relationships and transformation you are working to build. For instance, if you are working with several families on life skills development, at Christmas don't do angel trees for the kids in those families. Instead, offer a Christmas store where parents can buy gifts for their children at reduced costs and practice the skills they are learning, as well as maintain their dignity as providers in their households.

This kind of long-haul work is a significant shift for Matthean congregations. It is a significant shift for most congregations, and yet we should all be doing it. Mattheans may be frustrated by the time it takes to see change. To help a congregation adapt, consider studying a book with the mission or outreach team, such as *Toxic Charity* or *When Helping Hurts.* Taking a class or doing a study is an action that most Matthean churches can get behind.

Lukan Challenges

Primary Challenge: The Junior-High Syndrome

Junior high. Was there ever a time in your life when you knew exactly where you stood in the social order, and also knew you could not move out of the place you had been pigeon-holed? That's because it was a highly organized, highly stratified society defined by cliques.[1] You were a jock or a cheerleader or a nerd (sometimes specifically a band or choir or computer nerd), or a goth, and that is where you stayed. There was little to no intermixing among groups. That was junior high, and probably senior high too.

The greatest challenge Lukan churches face is forming cliques. Sometimes the church is small enough that it is one big clique, but it is a clique nonetheless. Lukans are highly relational people, but there are only so many people most of us are willing to get to know. Relationships take time and energy, and we are all limited in our time and energy. So at church, we like to just work on maintaining the relationships that have become very dear to us, rather than spending the time and energy to know someone else.

Just like junior high, one bully can hold the whole place hostage, because no one will want to challenge the bully. It will cause too much trouble. Lukans even fear losing their bullies, and bullies know it. But a church absolutely cannot grow and love new people in the grips of a bully.

Lukan churches proudly describe themselves as one of the friendliest churches around. You are. You are very friendly . . . to yourselves. Visitors to Lukan churches will frequently describe the congregation as friendly on the surface—Lukans are wonderful at creating a welcoming space—but impossible to break into. I experienced this first hand at a church while I

1. I am going to go ahead and admit that some of this understanding is defined by my Gen X experience. It is present in all generations, but Gen Z seems to have deliberately pushed against this reality, at least as I have watched my son experience it. But he would still know what I am talking about, so it hasn't disappeared altogether.

was in seminary. I was eager to be more involved there, and to get to know anyone beyond the handshake at the passing of the peace, so I tried to volunteer as a greeter. But I was told that I could not be a greeter because they also went out to dinner together, and they didn't have room for anyone else to go with them.

Lukans put a higher priority on their relationships than the mission Jesus gives us. The great irony there is that Jesus's mission is new relationships! Lukans could be the best at fulfilling the mission of loving God and neighbor, of making new disciples, which they will do as they love new people. Yet a Lukan community is frustrated about this. They have no more room at the table for anyone else. The places are all taken.

Primary Challenge Remedy: Break It Up!

Junior high is also grimly remembered as a time when fights broke out in the hallway. It can happen between cliques. However, a Lukan church will do everything it can to keep a fight from breaking out. Some Lukan churches seem to have "hall monitors" stationed everywhere! As a consequence, Lukan churches take few risks and spend forever talking through a decision; they don't want to lose anyone, so they will stand still to keep that from happening. They will wither and die rather than risk making someone mad.

Lukans should learn to make some people mad. You should disrupt the cliques. From time to time, your Lukan church should change things. It is the only way you make space for new people. And we are ordered to make space for new people! Jesus did not tell us go and make three or four disciples, and that will be good enough. Just think of the reality of the last words Jesus spoke in Luke–Acts: you have to build relationships all the way to the ends of the earth! That feels like a never-ending endeavor—because it is!

So how do Lukans keep from turning inward? Lukan churches insert intentional disruption. It's a risk for the Lukan pastor who aims to please.

So practice "de-cliquing." Not unilaterally. Lukans require conversation about how to do it. Here are a few ideas:

1. Swap Groups: Have a season when people intentionally move into different groups. For instance, if summer is a time when your attendance dips due to the unpredictability of vacations, combine two Sunday school classes into one. Or assign a third of every Sunday school class to go to a different class for a month once or twice a year. Mix it up!

2. Start New Groups: You should be doing this anyway. Lukan churches, though, do not like the idea of one of them leaving to go into a new group. It's necessary! During nine years at a church, I did not get to know anyone past a handshake until my last year when they started new small groups that met to discuss the sermon series. Most people will not be patient enough to be ignored (or deliberately excluded) by a church for years before they are integrated into a group. Start identifying the people who have a talent for welcoming new people, and name them as the people who will start new groups, and name the times when they will do that. For help identifying these folks, either look for significant extroverts, or use the Gospel Discipleship test to find a Matthean-Lukan or a Lukan-Matthean. Give him or her a checklist for how to start a new space (group or ministry team) and when. Or tell a Markan to pay attention to the movement of the Holy Spirit and bring a passion to start something new. A Markan's strength is to integrate all people.

3. Hire Spies: Part of the challenge is perspective. Lukan churches will not believe you if you tell them they are not really friendly. They *know* they are, because every time they come in the building they are so warmly received, and they so warmly receive others. This narrative is difficult to challenge, because it is the defining narrative for their identity. If they aren't friendly, then who are they? This is where lining up some mystery worshippers can be very helpful. Having people come in deliberately as visitors to assess how welcoming everything is, from the facilities to the people, and then sharing their experience, is an effective way to

challenge the friendly narrative. It works best if you can get some of these mystery worshippers to show up and share their experience in person. Lukans can dismiss a piece of paper. They really struggle to dismiss an actual person in front of them.

4. Get Out!: Lukans get very comfortable with the people they know. They also get very comfortable with how their familiars get along. That kills their motivation for including new people because those people can disrupt the equilibrium of the system. But the mission is to make new disciples. Lukans, then, should intentionally create spaces outside the church to do that. Sometimes meeting outside the church for new things acts as an intermediate step, because it keeps Lukans from trying to disrupt church as they know it. Another plus to this movement is that it actually does enact the instructions to go out to the "ends of the earth" (even if you only went as far as the local restaurant). To establish external relational spaces, obtain the resources for Fresh Expressions.[2]

5. Train Everyone as Greeters: If everyone is aware of the process of welcoming someone, and if everyone is trained for their respective roles, then a Lukan church is better prepared for making connections with people. Place greeters in the parking lot and at the doors. That is the first welcome, and it is simply a good greeting and offer of help to guide them where they need to go. Ushers can then welcome folks into the sanctuary. Then, each section of the sanctuary or worship space should have shepherds—people identified to pay attention to that section. Those shepherds do pay attention to who is usually there, including noting who is absent to follow up with them later that week, but not to the detriment of welcoming new folks. The shepherds should be the ones who take time to visit with the new folks. The goal of this visit is to glean information so you can to make follow-up contact possible, and to learn something about the guests that would help the shepherd connect them with someone

2. Audrey Warren and Kenneth H. Carter Jr., *Fresh Expressions: A New Kind of Methodist Church for People Not in Church* (Nashville: Abingdon Press, 2017) and Michael Beck with Jorge Acevedo, *A Field Guide to Methodist Fresh Expressions* (Nashville: Abingdon Press, 2020).

> else in the community. The last layer of greeting would be for everyone in the congregation to be prepared to have someone new sitting next to them, and ready to welcome them. Also, everyone in the church should be trained in how to be flexible enough to let someone sit in their pew and not get upset about it! Training everyone takes some of the anxiety out of welcoming guests, because it defines the process, and equips everyone for taking responsibility for welcoming others. And to do the training? Why not take a worship service every so often to teach awareness about others? That's when you have everyone there and in their places. Such training is organic, and it brings the whole congregation into the conversation.

Secondary Challenge: Paralysis

Lukans become anxious about one thing: losing people. Lukans will do practically anything to keep their community intact. This usually means Lukans avoid change and can become hostage to unhealthy behavior. Rather than risking a new vision for ministry, which may upset people who like things just like they are, Lukans will keep doing things the same old way. They assume this will keep everyone happy. That is a false assumption, but more importantly it paralyzes everyone's faith journey. It halts us from taking the next step we need to take on the path to Jesus. It is as if we are standing at a crossroads refusing to go any direction. But if we stay in that space, we will get hit by the next oncoming car.

In practice, Lukan churches will make some change even when motivated by fear. They will make the changes demanded by the loudest person. Lukans who lack clarity about their call to continue to move out and reach people in new ways will instead seek the comfort of those who are currently there. The loudest person, then, gets their way, which Lukans accept to keep the peace. Accommodation allows a bully to take hold. A bully in a Lukan church can hold a community hostage to that person's will, and God's desires for that people will be steamrolled.

Secondary Challenge Remedy: Fight the Good Fight

Lukans must learn how to fight. They should learn that conflict can be transformative. They need proof that disagreements can actually deepen relationships. It's helpful for Lukan communities to be trained in conflict resolution. Then, demonstrate that bullying behavior is damaging to the soul of the community and to the soul of the bully. Often a church bully is simply in the wrong church. If that is the case, the bully should be encouraged to leave if the bully can't grow spiritually in this faith community. When a church becomes addicted to keeping people happy, rather than a church dedicated to pleasing God, we are worshipping idols. We have missed the point when our meetings are about how we feel (comfortable, satisfied, mad, bored) about things, instead of asking who will this help us reach. We should shift our focus from self (self being everyone who is currently worshipping there) to others (people who need to know Jesus). Then we make decisions that include the ones who aren't there. This mind shift will make some of the in-group mad or uncomfortable. It will be hard. It may help a comfortable Lukan faith community to realize that individuals and faith communities are wired differently for discipleship. Some people need to leave to go somewhere else where they can better live into the person God is calling them to be. Your church can't be all things to all people, and God doesn't mean for it to try.

If it is any consolation, at a Lukan church, Lukans don't tend to actually leave. They may grumble a lot. But they don't often leave. Once new people are coming, and they get to know them and have new relationships, they tend to settle down. If a Lukan church refuses to make changes, though, they can count on one thing: the Markans, Mattheans, and Johannines will all eventually leave. So to keep the community intact, or more importantly to see it grow, Lukans need to get comfortable with change.

Johannine Challenges

Primary Challenge: Unchecked Tyranny

Since biblical times we have all observed a significant spiritual leader, who commands the attention and following of hundreds if not thousands of people, and then has a significant moral failure and a very public downfall. Or recall the faith community that turns into a cult, where the leader takes an entire flock into a destructive space. Or a pastor is able to abuse staff and congregants alike, feeding his or her own desires and ego while wrecking the faith of those he or she is supposed to shepherd.

None of these tragedies came out of nowhere. Most of them were preceded by tests of power. There were warning signs about a leader. Some behaviors send up obvious flags: isolating staff or certain parishioners, abusive outbursts in staff meetings, manipulative behavior. Many of these, however, start out as traits that parishioners admire and expect of their pastors: workaholism, being at the beck and call of all parishioners, not taking a vacation, being present at every single event at the church, and so on. Johannine churches also hand over an incredible amount of authority to their pastors. Johannine churches especially have a high view of their pastor, which comes with significant expectations, such that unhealthy behavior might be encouraged, and potentially inevitable.

Primary Challenge Remedy: Accountability and Shared Leadership

Johannine churches should put systems of accountability in place. The pastor needs a trusted group that can act as counsel for his or her ministry. These *peers* should be willing to tell the pastor no. If this group always pats the pastor on the back, then they may be encouraging dangerous behavior rather than preventing it. Feeding the pastor's ego constantly will inflate that pastor's self-worth. If you find yourself part of such a group, and begin to notice that this is the group's purpose, raise concerns in the group, and if that doesn't correct things, start raising concerns with other leadership in the church. To identify people who speak truth to a Johannine pastor, look to your Markans. If they feel empowered, they willingly call out behavior that is contrary to the Spirit.

And there should be other leadership in the church. Again, this leadership should not consist of the pastor's best friends. One of the strengths of a Johannine system is that it ought to be developing new leadership as more and more people are mentored and guided into significant ways of service. At its healthiest, a Johannine church should be sharing leadership across the congregation, even as it begins with very concentrated leadership at the top. The goal, though, is congregational development of mutual growth in following Jesus, not creating a bunch of people who are following the pastor. As leadership is shared across the congregation, the expectations on the pastor should also diminish.

Most Johannine pastors go into the ministry to serve, not to abuse people or engage in unhealthy and morally problematic behaviors. But the lure of power is strong. The exhaustion of ministry is significant. If called to help hold a pastor accountable, one of the first things you can do is make sure the pastor is honoring Sabbath (usually not on Sundays for pastors), that they are taking all of their vacation (and not using it to go to church conferences), that they are engaging in regular continuing education to renew their minds, and that they are making time for their families. All those things can contribute to a healthier spiritual leader, one who is less likely to crash and burn and take the whole church with them.

Secondary Challenge: Slow and Resented Discipleship

A Johannine discipleship system typically begins with the pastor spending a year mentoring a small group of leaders. The choice of leaders should be intentional, rather than taking from the first twelve people who volunteer. These leaders will then serve as mentors to other people, so they should be people who are gifted in leading and teaching and who are people the congregation admires already.

Though favoritism is avoided in the process, some people may be resentful. In part, people come to a Johannine church because they love learning from the pastor. Most Johannines would yearn for the opportunity to get personal instruction from someone they admire. While some people in the congregation won't view themselves worthy of such attention, many others will.

The second challenge for a Johannine system is its slow growth. If it takes a year to train the first round of mentors, then by the second year there is impact upon the congregation. Depending on how many disciples each mentor can guide, by end of the second year there can be as many as 144 to 156 people who have been mentored. Still, some people may become restless or disinterested in the opportunity, because they don't see how it fits their lives.

Secondary Challenge Remedy: Transparency

The best way to deal with this challenge is to be honest about it, and make it inclusive and diverse where you can. The first group that the pastor works with should come from congregational nominations. That inhibits the system from perceptions that the pastor has a secret club.

When introducing this pathway to a congregation filled with eager learners, feel free to diagram how it will unfold, and to help people see the vision of the future. As you are explaining the value of mentor-apprentice relationships, however, also take the opportunity to encourage the people of the congregation to move ahead and work on such relationships themselves. If you admire someone's understanding of scripture, ask that person to meet with you for a few weeks to read the Bible together. Encourage them to share their gifts on social media, and then as you see a gift you would like to cultivate, reach out to that person and see if they can show you how. You might even have a mentor-apprentice posting board for your congregation. Then you have opened up the system more. It allows for more organic development of the culture of discipleship you are trying to cultivate.

Chapter Five

WORSHIP CHARACTERISTICS FOR EACH TYPE

When we understand how our church is like one or more of the four earliest Christian faith communities, we can bring our worship in line so that it reflects our discipleship. This move allows us to emphasize our discipleship pathways in the moment when the majority of us gather together to sing and proclaim our faith. Here we don't have space to discuss style of music, though some correlations might be made between type of faith community and traditional, contemporary, blended, modern, jazz, bluegrass, R&B, rock, grunge, global, and contemplative music genres. This chapter instead will discuss what other elements should be present in worship to encourage people to live their discipleship in the midst of the central practice of the Christian faith.

Some readers are thinking, "Oh, we can't change worship. The whole congregation will revolt!" However, you will probably find that most of these recommendations are already at work in some way in your church. Your worship probably already reflects your discipleship tendencies, because people have probably already asked for many of these things. If some recommendation for adjustment to your worship practice would make sense, in light of who you are as an intentional faith community, you now have a framework (Gospel Discipleship) for a conversation. This framework can mitigate feelings that worship change is driven by the pastor's personal preference or cultural background. To be fair, personal preference for a well-trained pastor is usually learned, remembered, and absorbed through a theological tradition. Self-awareness about both worship tradition and discipleship type is one way to clear the fog on the pathways for the disciples in your church.

Pastors test to find out their discipleship type too, and their type will most likely influence how they introduce transitions to worship. Lukans will likely collaborate with a worship committee or team, and will probably be intentional about communicating changes well in advance, to have an opportunity to hear from others. Mattheans will try to take action relatively quickly, but how that unfolds will likely depend largely on what their secondary gift is as well as how they understand church. Markans probably want to change worship all the time, so they would do well to educate their people about spontaneity and impulse. Markans can defer style to the dominant tendency of their congregation, but use special Sundays or seasonal transitions for more out-of-the box worship experiences. Johannine pastors have already lined worship up the way they want it. This chapter will probably help them understand why they do this, and perhaps help their churches understand too.

Markan Worship

The best way to describe Markan worship is to say that as soon as you describe it, you should be ready to change it. Markans are creative people who assume that the Holy Spirit is moving in new and different ways. They would have the same expectations of worship. You can have the ancient basic pattern of worship with Markans, but let it be a base from which variety springs up.

While Matthean worship is highly participatory, Markan worship may be the same, but in this case the emphasis is not on making sure everyone is doing something. This time the emphasis is on making sure that those who do something are expressing their God-given gifts. Markans want people with special gifts to have an opportunity to share those gifts. Do you have dancers in your congregation? Then integrate liturgical dance from time to time. Do you have gifted musicians? Make sure they get in the rotation to offer their gift to God. Do you have painters or potters? Try allowing them to paint or spin up what they hear as the pastor delivers a sermon.

Markan spaces should also reflect such creativity. Spend time with altar design in a Markan church, and change it out regularly. Let it organically reflect the seasons, or the sermon series, or the life of the community. Unleash the gifts in your congregation to help that happen. Markans will resonate with the changing expression of the power of God. Also, consider doing prayer stations, but again, let those stations adapt and change around the needs and gifts of the community. Markan worship spaces need to be as flexible as possible to accommodate the movement of the Spirit and the people, to allow for a wide variety of creative expressions before God.

Prayer is a critical practice for Markan churches, because Markans need to make space to hear the Holy Spirit. And since hearing is more important than speaking, integrate significant periods of silence in a Markan congregation. Give people the opportunity to hear God's Spirit speak to them. Of course, with some Markan congregations you may experience gifts such as speaking in and interpreting tongues, if that is a gift the congregation has nurtured. Any Markan congregation has potential for that capacity. Markan worship is intentional about making space for the unplanned and unpredictable act of praise to happen. Charismatic expressions are deeply reflective of Markan communities.

Markans will be less attached to worship remaining the same from week to week. Markans will grow bored and restless with such worship. It will feel like there is not enough opportunity to express the variety of gifts in a congregation, and it will feel like the voice of the Spirit has stopped speaking if things come to a standstill for too long. Allow worship to change in order, structure, and expression to fit the movement of the Spirit. Markan pastors can plan worship long term, because again the Spirit appreciates preparation. A good Markan pastor, however, will plan deliberate disruption and be ready to have her own plans adapted or thrown out along the way.

Matthean Worship

Since Mattheans are disciples of action, Matthean worship should be highly participatory. Every person gathered in the body should be invited to participate in some way. This could be by standing and singing a song. It could be in unison prayer. Many of the standardized worship practices of a typical church will encourage a Matthean disciple.

Matthean congregations are encouraged to step it up a notch and make sure that many opportunities to serve are available in worship. Do you have laypeople who serve as liturgists? Do they lead the prayers, read scripture, present announcements, and more? How many other ways to serve in worship are present? How open are the opportunities to join in the musical options?

Movement is also important for a Matthean community, but movement that makes sense for their context. Movement from standing to sitting to kneeling in a Catholic context would make sense for Catholic Mattheans. Mattheans in more evangelical traditions may feel more comfortable with movements like sitting and standing, or lifting hands up during prayers or singing. Some congregations may integrate movement in prayer, similar to sign language, to open up the bodily experience in other moments of worship, or they may put in prayer stations or invite people to kneel before the altar. Matthean people don't like to sit still for too long. Ideally their worship spaces should be designed to allow the movement that moves the people.

Pastors should be encouraged to integrate a call to action in their service as well. One pastor, who learned his congregation was Matthean, suddenly popped up in the midst of our discussion about their type and said, "You know what just occurs to me? The sermon series that went over the best here was the one that I did where I gave them homework. They loved that!" Of course they did! He gave Mattheans something to do. So if a sermon calls people to action, or if a call to action is given just before or as part of the benediction, Mattheans will leave worship with a sense of purpose. Matthean communities could also look at integrating such actions into worship. Perhaps from time to time worship can be organized around a particular mission project that actually takes place within the worship space.

Finally, Mattheans will especially resonate with taking attendance and being held accountable to it. Give them a box to check that allows them to let you know that they were there. Track how often they have been there, and then let them know by sending them updates. Help them keep track of the actions they take, and help them know that you notice all that they do.

Lukan Worship

Some congregations won't give up their time for joys and concerns or their time for passing the peace. Those are probably Lukan congregations. Lukans need ample opportunities for fellowship within a worship service. You also probably need to plan for greater than average time spent on any of those moments. Lukans are not going to stand up, briefly shake hands with the three people in their immediate vicinity, and then sit back down ready to worship again. They are going to move across the church, trying to say hello to as many people as possible, or they are going to get in a deep conversation with the person next to them and get all caught up on that person's life this past week. Connecting with each other is as important to a Lukan congregation as connecting to God is in worship. Lukans come to worship to solidify both relationships.

Lukans love the opportunity to share their stories, especially among those they trust and love. Allowing space for someone to share how God has moved in his or her life the prior week will serve the dual purpose of helping Lukans practice conversation about God with others and allow them to grow in love and vulnerability with each other. The pastor can decide whether these moments should be screened in advance or not. When introducing the practice of sharing God moments, open the floor because often people are shy about such work, but they want to share their lives with each other. It probably won't cross boundaries.

Especially if you are not in a small Lukan church, you may need ways of developing small communities within the larger one in the worship space. You can take advantage of the fact that we are all creatures of habit. Lukans especially tend to gravitate to the people they know, and regardless of type we all tend to sit in the same pew from week to week. Many larger churches train people to be hosts for sections of pews. They check in with everyone each week, and welcome anyone new who has chosen to sit in their area. They notice who has come back after an absence. The effect is creating smaller communities within the larger communities. These are concentric circles in action.

Lukan churches may also want to look at how they organize their worship space. Does the space allow for and encourage fellowship? Some churches have removed pews to put in "praygrounds," spaces where children are encouraged to play during the service, or coffee bars where people can gather and chat. Some have moved to table seating, which allows people to look across and see each other. Some keep stationary furniture such as pews but set them at angles so people can see each other more easily. Lukans won't typically be drawn to a dark space. They like to be able to see their people. Lukan churches should look at the value of interactive and inclusive space as a place to live into relationship building. Such churches should also place God at the center of their worship space, sometimes quite literally in the placement of an altar, because they will also want to live into deep relationship with God as well. If you have the opportunity to build a new sacred space, think seriously about curved options (half or full circles or octagons). Reflect your concentric circles of movement through those we love to those we seek to love in the creation of our holy space.

Johannine Worship

It's easy to recognize a Johannine church, at least when it was built. The pulpit will be dead center. In a Johannine church the sermon will be at least thirty minutes of the service. Now, that doesn't mean all churches with a pulpit at the center are Johannine, or that all churches with a thirty-minute sermon are Johannine (though on that one, bet that the pastor is probably Johannine).[1] But all Johannine churches should have both of those elements. That is, if they have a pulpit in the first place. If they do not have a pulpit, count on the pastor preaching from the center of the people, however that is set up. Johannine worship organizes in a very Protestant manner—the sermon is the heart of worship. Why? Because that is the moment when people are focused around learning from two great teachers: the Bible and the preacher.

Worship is a great opportunity for teaching and equipping the community. So each element of the worship service, from song choice to benediction, underscores what is to be learned that day. Johannine pastors are likely to insist on tight coordination with all those who have responsibility for elements of the service. A Johannine pastor may insist on designing the whole service, unless they take their mentoring role seriously when working with worship leaders. Johannine pastors "preside" and typically want final say on the purpose and expression of worship.

Johannine worship has high expectations of those who help lead it. Everyone up front should be an expert. Johannine churches will have worship professionals. The people who lead are assumed to have credentials, even if the credentials are granted by the community. This is not the place

1. Many churches design their spaces based on trends at the time their church was built. Putting thought into reflecting the theology of the church or the way the people want to exhibit their discipleship has not always been a consideration. Thus, it is not unusual since the Protestant Reformation to place the pulpit at the center, because the reformers were teachers.

for random volunteers. If there are volunteers, they have been mentored into the roles they play. Johannine churches may make use of occasional guest experts. These can be guest preachers of course, but they can also be testimonies of significant leaders in the church and community. Johannine churches love good teaching. Some variety in source is at times appreciated. Most Johannine churches put their faith in the teaching of their senior pastor.

Scripture is also at the heart of Johannine worship, since God's word is the other great teacher. Johannine churches may stand for the reading of the Gospel or may bring in the Bible in a procession. These churches will also likely be protective of their preferred translation. Use of another translation needs a good reason. Johannine churches may have a significant altar Bible, and people may actually read from it! In some traditions, parishioners may bring their Bibles with them and read from them too. Or they may use the Bibles provided in the pews.

Architecturally, the standard cross-shaped, long central line (a basilica) that points to the pulpit works fine. So can other arrangements, if the pulpit is at the center. Unlike Lukan churches, lighting can be turned toward the pulpit. Johannine people appreciate architecture that lines their focus toward the teaching and toward the professionals leading worship. Healthy Johannine churches, though, will also find a prominent central place for the altar, as Johannine churches sometimes need physical reminders that they worship the Word of God (Jesus), not the word of God (scripture and teaching/preaching).

How to Integrate Multiple Types

Every Sunday a particular church makes this announcement in worship: "You will probably find that 75 percent of this service resonates with you. The other 25 percent is for the people sitting next to you." This is a reminder that in worship we are bringing the whole community before

God, and sometimes one is not going to sense the relevance, but then someone else probably does. Give thanks for that.

As your church is learning and living into your Gospel Discipleship type, you will notice that one type does not apply to everyone. You probably have a type that syncs with the majority, but does not capture the rich diversity of your people. So how do you organize worship in the midst of difference?

Your leadership should take this up for discernment. One suggestion is similar to what a Markan pastor would do if serving in a non-Markan church. Default to your faith community's dominant type, but use special Sundays to experiment with other ways of worshipping. Further, if you have a dominant type but a strong secondary type, blend your worship to include elements of both. For instance, if you are in a Johannine-Markan church, make sure you include significant times of silent prayer. That allows people to listen to the voice of God, but also fits with the focused aims of a Johannine service. If you are in a Lukan-Matthean church, doing an occasional mission project during worship allows for people to visit while they work.

Most congregations are not in a place financially or emotionally to make significant changes to the worship space. But think creatively about what you could do. If you are in a Matthean church and you have no way to kneel before the altar, could someone create a movable kneeler that can be brought in, or added to a prayer station at the side? If you are a Lukan church who has the altar fenced around by such kneelers, blocking people from direct access to God, consider removing the kneelers or move it to a prayer station at the side. Are you a Markan community trying to worship from pews lined up in rows aiming at the front? Consider scheduling some worship to take place outside or at another location in the community. We are created in the image of a creative creator God. Use your God-given creative minds to consider what options are available so that your worship more meaningfully brings your people in love and adoration before God.

Chapter Six

PASTORS OF EACH TYPE

Church leaders benefit from understanding how pastors of each type tend to operate. Most people typically have a strong primary and secondary type. Rarely is there a pastor with a three- or four-way tie on the test, and so far only one pastor with a single type. Most pastors have a primary and secondary tendency, and will lean into both readily.

Markan Pastors

Markan pastors are enthusiastic vessels of God's power. As a container, they recognize that they are meant to hold God's power only long enough to let it overflow and fill the cups of others. These pastors, then, resist hierarchies, preferring instead to share leadership across the congregation. Markan pastors are highly creative, typically energetic people. They are spontaneous, out-of-the-box thinkers. Markans are ministry innovators. They will try things no one else has imagined trying. They also love to empower their people. They can see gifts in people that other pastors may have missed, and they will encourage their people to develop those gifts. If they are deeply plugged into the Spirit, they will seem to have otherworldly inspiration when it comes to identifying who should head a new ministry, or what direction the church needs to move next.

Markan pastors, like Markans generally, almost seem to have spiritual ADD. Their attention does not hold in one place long. Or perhaps it is more accurate to say that their attention will only hold in one place as long as it is necessary for them to stay attentive. If they feel a ministry or program has outlived its usefulness, they will want to do away with it immediately, or at the very least they will stop backing up that ministry either with their time or the church's resources. They may also, however, turn their attention away from a ministry because they feel they have put the right people in charge of it. They trust their people. They trust the Spirit has gifted those people to do what needs to be done for the reign of God. So do not take a Markan pastor's withdrawal from a ministry personally. Actually, take it (especially if resources keep flowing that way) as a deep vote of confidence.

Unless they are also Lukan or Matthean, and visits are on their to-do list, Markan pastors will not be enthusiastic about long-term visitation and pastoral care. They may do remarkably well with hospital visits, because those are short-term care needs. Sustained visitation of the homebound or those who are in nursing homes can be a struggle for Markans. When they do visit, it will most likely be a spur-of-the-moment, happen to be in the neighborhood, kind of thing. Markans do also tend to know crucial times to visit, though. They get a nudge of the Spirit. As for routine pastoral care needs, Markans can be remarkable at short-term needs, like premarital counseling, but for longer-term needs (especially if they know that counseling is not their gift) they will definitely refer you to someone else. When they are healthy and self-aware, they are good at maintaining boundaries. One Markan pastor described his work like this: "I am a cracked vase. I can take in whatever people pour into me, but I let it flow out of the cracks and move on." Yet Markan pastors are also good at identifying the people in their community who are gifted at such care. Markan pastors do well to organize a pastoral-care committee, training them to make visits and keep in contact with the pastor so that the pastor is better about knowing when a personal visit is needed. Don't mistake this delegation of duties to others as a sign that Markans lack love for their people. They deeply love them, both those who need care and those who are good at care, and they want to bring those two groups who really need each other together. It is a selfless act on the part of Markans that sometimes gets interpreted as laziness, lack of caring, or utter selfishness.

Markan pastors are not good at long-term strategic thinking for a church. A Markan pastor who comes into a church that already has a clear vision is very likely to just ride that vision out, especially if she thinks the vision still fits the aims of the Spirit. A Markan pastor who does not feel the vision fits is more likely to stop emphasizing it, but will not replace it with anything else. Markan pastors instead are more likely to have short-term emphases, such as giving the church a central theme for a season. As a Markan, I once gave a church a theme to work through for a year: "Love One Another." It was because I knew that church had some past hurt that it needed healing around. But I also recognized that once we had done intentional healing we would need to move to the next thing. It was a temporary vision for a temporary need. The exception to Markan pastors and strategic thinking are Markans who have a strong Matthean or Johannine secondary. Those pastors may in fact identify a vision. However, they are also not likely to seek a great deal of input from the community on what that vision should be. They will assume that the Spirit gave it to them to lead the community into. A Lukan church may struggle with what seems like a dictatorial strategy.

Markan pastors typically don't want to stay anywhere too long. If a Markan pastor is serving a Markan church, the fit could persist, and then an accountability group needs to remain attentive to whether the church is tipping too deep in the direction of their challenges. They can become so confident in their ability to tap into the Spirit that they tap into their own desires instead. Otherwise, a Markan pastor's usefulness in one location is like the wind. It is nice to have a breeze for a while, but eventually everyone grows weary of being whipped around. Markans will help churches push the envelope of what church could and should be, and are great at disturbing the peace, so to speak. They help congregations that are stymied and who have lost their creativity move from their stuck place. There comes a time, though, when a non-Markan congregation will finally say, "Enough is enough. Let's settle down and catch our breath for a minute." A strong Markan pastor, who honestly couldn't push the congregation as much as desired, will also be weary of containing the energy. A new place to experiment will be pursued. So let Markan pastors move around in short bursts. It will be good for the church as a whole to let Markans do that. Let the Spirit move where the Spirit will.

Matthean Pastors

Matthean pastors are hardworking disciples of Jesus Christ. They are the movers and shakers of the ministry world. They are in constant motion. They are busy all the time. Matthean pastors are driven to do all they can for Jesus in all the time they have.

Matthean pastors are good at strategic thinking for their churches, and the missions and visions tends to be very action based. Depending on their secondary wing, they can be highly collaborative with strategic thinking (if they are secondarily Lukan), or may come up with it virtually on their own but be good at herding the people into it (if they are secondarily Johannine). If they are secondarily Markan, their tendency to be collaborative will depend largely on how the Spirit directs them and whether they identify some of their people as gifted strategic thinkers.

Mattheans can be very structured and organized in how they perform ministry. Anything perceived as a duty of a pastor, you can count on a Matthean to get it done. Mattheans will experience conflict with their congregations if a Matthean pastor's expectations of the office are significantly different from the expectations of the people. For this reason, it is important for Mattheans to have early and frequent conversations with key leaders about expectations and boundaries in ministry. A seasoned Matthean pastor will probably have learned personal limitations and can share those honestly with the church. A greener Matthean pastor will try to fulfill both personal expectations and the expectations of the people. This tendency makes Mattheans highly subject to burnout.

Mattheans tend to struggle with overextending themselves, because in part they are very good at getting things done. They get enormous satisfaction in action. If there is something to do, they want to do it. They will be right in the thick of practically everything that their church and their people are doing. They may, in fact, be leading the people into action most of the time. Honoring Sabbath could be a spiritual struggle for Matthean pastors, unless they intentionally put it on their to-do list. Even then, if something else comes along that seems more urgent and important, or that Mattheans think will do more good in either the short or long term, they are likely to sacrifice their own well-being instead. Mattheans need someone who can hold them accountable to rest.

Lukan Pastors

Lukan pastors are highly relational servants of God, because they will pay attention to the needs of others, often over and above their own spiritual needs. Their people are dear to them.

Lukan pastors are likely to develop their ministry in the concentric circles described for Lukan individuals and congregations. They will nurture deep relationships with an inner circle of people in the center of anywhere they serve. Lukans don't intend to be exclusionary when doing this, but they need a trusted group of people they can love deeply and that they know loves them deeply to sustain their ministry. Lukan pastors will also put significant emphasis on the love and care of the wider congregation. They will be gifted at visiting the sick. Indeed, they will be gifted at visiting everyone. These pastors will go to the sporting events of the youth in their church and sit in the bleachers chatting with their people. They may hang out longer at wedding receptions than most pastors (unless the presence of a pastor is disrupting the fun of the place, and then they will leave for the good of the party). Lukan pastors will make sure their people are cared for and know they are loved. Then, once that base is well established, they will move out into the community. However, that move will be deliberate. Lukan pastors will not typically flit from location to location getting to know everyone in town (unless they are secondarily Matthean and feel like that is what they are supposed to do, or secondarily Markan and feel like the Spirit is directing them that way). They are more likely to become deeply involved in a space, like becoming a consistent presence at an elementary school as a volunteer or joining a few key community organizations that meet regularly around a shared goal that either reflects the goals of their congregations or themselves. These pastors are also the ones who will hang out at the coffee shop to shoot the breeze with people. Wherever they go, they will show up consistently, and their intention will be to get to know more people. Then, they will walk beside those people until they can walk them to a relationship with Jesus.

Like Markans, Lukan pastors will not be deeply interested in strategic thinking for a church. They will instead carry a consistent mission with them from church to church, and that will be a mission of helping people grow in love and relationship with Jesus Christ and each other. Lukans recognize that no matter where they go, the process for that mission is the same: invest time and attention in the people around you. Lukan pastors do well at smaller churches where they can get to know everyone deeply, or in larger churches with more intimate mechanisms of relationships, like a strong small group culture. Growth under a Lukan pastor would be slow and steady. They tend not to lose people, and if they do it tends to deeply grieve them. However, because they are so intentional in developing relationships, growth is an incremental process. Unless they are serving in a Lukan church that is helping carry the burden of integration of new people, growth will only occur at the pace that the pastor can develop new relationships.

As long as a Lukan pastor feels loved and feels love to give, the pastor will be content to stay in the same place to serve for a long time. Because

Lukan pastors become attached so early, they may struggle to see when it is time to move on. Pastoral moves are very hard on Lukans. Even if they don't feel the love of the people, Lukans will not want to give up on their flock. Just as Lukan churches become too attached to who they are, Lukan pastors can become too attached to serving a particular group of people. They need to be reminded from time to time that there are more people out there who need their love.

Johannine Pastors

Johannine pastors are strong shepherds of God's flock. Shepherd is an apt image for a Johannine, because Johannines feel they are responsible for the nurture and life of their sheep. They also tend to stand a bit removed from their people, with an overall vantage point of seeing the whole and also seeing any threats coming from a distance. They understand themselves as responsible for feeding the flock. Sermon preparation will consume Johannine pastors (some spend fifteen to twenty hours a week in preparation), because they see this as the central time when the most people gather around to be fed.

They build churches that flow outward from leadership. These churches tend to seem very hierarchical or corporate in nature. The best Johannine pastors, though, see this structure not in terms of the centralization of power but in terms of efficient ways of encouraging mentor-apprentice relationships. Johannines see everyone ultimately as pointed toward the feet of Jesus, and they will encourage everyone to see Jesus as their Lord and master. All are bowed to Christ, and thus all are on the same level in that sense. Johannines are realistic in their understanding that some people are closer to the feet of Jesus than others are. The goal, though, is to move everyone in that direction.

Johannines will be strong at leadership development. It is the core of their identity. They have trained as leaders of the church, and they take the responsibility of training others seriously. They will want this to be deep work. They will take a small group of people and walk them deeply through the scriptures. They will have a strong sense of the theology that people should embrace, and they will actively teach people about that theology. These pastors might anchor themselves in 1 Timothy to help them better understand their role and the kind of people they should be developing. For this reason, many Johannine pastors also see mentoring young or up-and-coming pastors as important to their work.

Because they are themselves strong leaders, they can also articulate a compelling mission and vision for a church. Compelling is the emphasis because Johannines see themselves as the central expert, so if they consult anyone they are likely to consult a limited and trusted initial group of leaders whom they mentored. Those people may or may not be able to challenge such a pastor's idea. A Johannine pastor is less likely to brainstorm with a group of people than to come in with an already significantly formed idea and seek input from there. The exceptions would be one with a Markan or Lukan secondary gift. Johannine-Mattheans are likely to see input as slowing down the process.

Johannine pastors are also gifted teachers. They may do it well one-on-one or with a large group. They can often adjust the teaching on the fly (especially if they are secondarily Markan) to meet the needs of the learners. Because they envision their role as experts, they have a wealth of knowledge from which to draw when they teach. They will tend not to teach on a subject they do not feel deeply prepared for, so Johannine pastors will draw regularly from their comfort zones. They may sometimes sound like a broken record, especially if they are not regularly challenging themselves to grow.

Fortunately, the healthiest Johannine pastors are lifelong learners. They recognize that to be able to serve as an example, to lead and teach their people, they must be constantly challenging themselves to grow. It is critical that a Johannine pastor take time for continuing education. Someone in the congregation (or several) should check in on the pastor's learning. For instance, ask whether he has read anything new lately, or attended a conference, or been in an online webinar.

Isolation is a danger for a Johannine pastor, because as the lone leader of a sea of people, the pastor will take on too much responsibility for the whole. If everything in the church points in the pastor's direction, Johannine pastors are subject to corruptions of power. When the church turns toward a cult of personality, and this happens at some megachurches, there is a problem. We are meant to worship Jesus, not our pastor. All pastors are subject to the temptation to making church about themselves, but Johannine pastors are particularly susceptible simply because of how they conceive of discipleship. Healthy churches will build significant systems of accountability to guard their pastors against this possibility. They should also recognize that Johannine pastors are the most adept at getting around such systems.

APPENDIX: APPLICATION

I haven't actually taken the Gospel Discipleship test, because I formulated the questions and answers. It would be difficult not to influence the results. So I have sat a long time with those questions. I have personally scored many of the tests. I have counseled individuals, small groups, and churches. And so, I can confidently say that I am a Markan-Johannine pastor.

I am Markan. If I have a default person of the Trinity, it is the Holy Spirit. You will frequently hear me talk about how the Spirit is empowering us to be the people God is calling us to be. I genuinely believe that the Spirit gifts people for the mission before them. I regularly take spiritual gifts tests, and while my top gifts tend to stay the same, the absolute top two alternate among my top five gifts based on where I am and how I am serving. I am Johannine largely due to having been deeply shaped by study. I have spent thirty-three years in school in my lifetime, not counting the years I have served as a teacher.

The two churches I served before coming to the Arkansas Conference offices for the United Methodist Church were Lukan-Matthean churches. A pastor can serve a church even when the pastor and the church are different types. It can generate some creative energy. However, it helps if everyone is aware that there are distinct differences at work. When I served two Fort Smith churches, this Gospel Discipleship model was not yet developed. The result was some success, as well as some significant missteps.

One of the two churches had been talking about doing a sanctuary renovation for at least twenty years. The struggle they had, however, was making specific decisions about the space. I see now that this struggle was due to the Lukan vein in them. There were people still in that congregation who had literally built, with their own hands, that sanctuary space. The congregation did not want to devalue that work (which might feel like devaluing those people) by altering the space, even though it desperately needed an update. The congregation had also raised enough money to update the flooring, but they could not make a decision on what type of flooring to go with—tile or carpet—because different people wanted different things. They had just about decided to put two different kinds of flooring in the same space.

The Johannine in me stepped in to take a central role in this process. Despite the fact that I had never renovated such a space, I am a student and could do the work to become enough of an expert to push it through. I also knew enough to invite experts in. This included a carpenter from within the congregation, as well as a flooring expert from without. When we invited experts in, we discovered that there was in fact a type of flooring that met the needs of both the tile and the carpet contingency (it is called carpet tile, and I highly recommend it for such spaces). When it came to design of such a space, I had my own creative design that I shared with the people, but more importantly I recognized (and so did the trustees) that there was a small group of women with passion for how the space could look. With the trustees' guidance, I unleashed them to make the critical decisions of color and coordination. The Spirit was definitely at work, because the decisions were rapid and unanimous.

Something in me must have recognized, though, that this highly relational and active church needed to be involved in this work on an intimate level. So, much of the work was done by the people of the congregation, not only echoing who they are but who they were. Some of the same families who had built the original sanctuary helped in the renovation. Also, there was one highly controversial decision to make: chairs or pews.

In that case, we had a church-wide conversation. Yes, it got heated. Yes, it went on for over two hours. At the end, though, everyone who wanted to speak had a chance to speak. The family came out intact once all was said and done. Through the course of the renovation, we lost not a single family. Yes, some people argued that I had been a little too prominent in the process, but people loved the new space, and they did acknowledge that they had actually accomplished a long-discussed goal.

As for the misstep, that came from leaning too heavily into my Markan side and assuming more people experienced God in that same way. In the other church, we had a worship service that stalled out and was not growing. Over one summer, we tried some experiential worship services in all our worship services, and we had more visitors during that series than any other stretch during my time there. I loved the variety and creativity of those services, so I proposed that we move the struggling worship service to that format. For me, it was an opportunity to move at a moment's notice toward the energy of the Holy Spirit. For relational people, however, it was far too disruptive to their comfort. They needed something more predictable. If I had understood better why I was in love with that format and they were not, we could have made some adjustments. Instead, I was moved to another position, and the pastor who followed me was left to pick up the scattered pieces.

As I worked with churches and reflected on my personal experience, I noticed that rarely are churches and pastors perfectly matched in their discipleship types. Such diversity is in fact God's design. Having only one type in common, or having all different types, keeps churches and pastors from standing too still. It also provides a means for recognizing each other's gifts and challenging each other's weaknesses. For that to work, however, mutual understanding is needed. Then, the next step is to make room for each other.

In the development of this Gospel Discipleship system, I worked with a pastor and the two congregations he served. One of his churches tested Matthean primarily, Lukan secondarily. The other church tested

Lukan primarily, Johannine secondarily. He tested Johannine primarily, Matthean secondarily. So he had one gift in common with each of his churches. But his lead gift was not the lead gift of either.

When I met with him and each of the churches, we were able to talk through what that meant. I shared with both that their pastor was likely to come into every meeting with a clear direction and path for where they needed to go next. As a Johannine, he would expect that of himself. As a secondary Matthean, his plans would most likely be highly action based. That fit remarkably well at the church that was primarily Matthean. They love assignments and checklists, and he was readily able to provide those. While the other church respected his command and expertise, they needed to know he loved them before they would be open to his direction. So we put expectation on the table. We talked through how they develop relationships, and we began to unpack how they understand love. He committed to making more space for conversation (as that was how they primarily developed relationships), but they committed to recognizing that conversation cannot go on forever; eventually you move on the things you talk about. In both cases, simply having the understanding of how everyone was operating allowed them to work together in a way that might better glorify God and honor the gifts of all at the table.

For churches who call their pastors, taking this test as a congregation will give you clarity about who you are, and inviting potential candidates to take it as well will give you clarity about the kind of leader she or he will be. In appointive systems, such information could be used as part of the discernment process of who to send where. Don't assume that you need to find matching types and send everyone where they match perfectly. That may work in some cases, but in others, everyone will be too comfortable. Pastor and church may settle in quickly and begin to default heavily toward the challenging aspects of their type. So while this Gospel Discipleship model can provide illumination on how everyone operates, it still takes deep prayer and discernment to seek God's will for a particular people.

GOSPEL DISCIPLESHIP TYPE ASSESSMENT

With each of the questions below, choose the ONE answer that you think BEST answers the question FOR YOU. You will most likely agree that more than one, perhaps even all, of the options is true, but choose the one that you think is the best response in your own opinion. The only wrong choice is a choice that does not reflect what you think.

1. Which of these words best describes discipleship to you?

    a. Empowering
    b. Doing
    c. Loving
    d. Learning

2. Which feels most like discipleship to you?

    a. Initiating a new ministry for Jesus that uses my specific gifts and graces
    b. Serving those who are hungry or thirsty
    c. Sitting with someone who is going through a hard time
    d. Learning about the Bible from a great teacher

3. What could best help you understand your faith and how to live it?
    a. A spiritual gifts test and a conversation with someone who can help me discern the results
    b. A basic inquiry class on the vows of membership at your church
    c. A small-group discussion
    d. Meeting with a trusted leader or pastor to talk about purpose (e.g., God's will)

4. What is the best witness to your personal faith?
    a. Living an authentic, faithful life
    b. Doing mission work so people see Jesus in my actions
    c. Spending time paying attention to other people and loving them
    d. Leading through Christ's example

5. Who would you most want to trade places with in the Bible?
    a. One of the disciples when the Holy Spirit shows up on Pentecost (Acts 2)
    b. The Good Samaritan who rescues the traveler assaulted on the side of the road (Luke 10)
    c. One of the people walking on the road to Emmaus with Jesus (Luke 24)
    d. The woman at the well who gets to talk one-on-one with Jesus (John 4)

6. What works best to help you grow in your faith?
    a. Having the freedom to figure out my own path
    b. A defined list of things to work on
    c. Collaborating with friends on how to grow
    d. Receiving direction from a trusted mentor

7. What is the biggest strength of your particular church?

a. We make space for all kinds of people
b. We have incredible programs and outreach
c. We have wonderful fellowship with each other
d. We offer solid and useful teaching on the Bible

8. What would you like people to say about your particular church?

a. People figure out their life's purpose here
b. People here are the hands and feet of Christ
c. We do life together well
d. Each person matters to us

9. What adjective best describes you?

a. Creative
b. Hardworking
c. Caring
d. Knowledgeable

10. Which word bests describes ideal leaders in a church?

a. Innovators
b. Organizers
c. Companions
d. Mentors

11. Which phrase best describes your ideal pastor?

a. Encourages and empowers the people
b. Casts a compelling vision that gets us moving
c. Walks alongside us through life
d. Excellent teacher and preacher

12. What is the best way to make a disciple?

    a. Cultivate personal gifts to live fully into the person God calls them to be
    b. Engage in mission and worship together
    c. Build a meaningful relationship that encourages growth through sharing faith with each other
    d. Teach the biblical principles of discipleship (e.g., studying the parables or Sermon on the Mount)

13. What would be a significant faith crisis for you?

    a. If I felt like the Spirit had left me or my church
    b. If I felt like my church wasn't doing anything to change lives
    c. If my Sunday school class or small group got in a fight and dissolved
    d. If my pastor or mentor had a significant moral failure

14. What do you think the purpose of the church is in the twenty-first century?

    a. Helping people recognize and cultivate the gifts God has given them
    b. Making a difference in our community in the name of Jesus
    c. Providing space for people to develop authentic, loving relationships with Christ and each other
    d. Teaching people how to live like Jesus

15. Which phrase best describes who faithful people of God are?

    a. People who know who they are and whose they are
    b. People who are transforming the world for Christ
    c. People who love God and love neighbor
    d. People who follow Jesus

16. When the church is off track, . . .

    a. People quit contributing—no one wants to share their gifts with a broken community
    b. No one's life is being changed for the better
    c. People quit caring about each other
    d. The leadership tends to get in trouble

17. To grow in my own discipleship, I need . . .

    a. The chance to start a new ministry that God has laid on my heart
    b. To do something—engage in Bible study, help lead in worship, or go on a mission trip—that will move me out of my comfort zone
    c. To open my home and my heart to a new small group of people
    d. To spend some time learning from the wise people of faith in our congregation

18. The church should . . .

    a. Pay attention to how the Holy Spirit is moving in its midst
    b. Teach people how to go into the world and make a difference in people's lives
    c. Build a supportive and loving community
    d. Be an example for the rest of the world

19. The church is missing the point when . . .

    a. It isn't allowing people to use their gifts to serve God
    b. It isn't making a difference in the community
    c. It isn't getting to know its neighbors
    d. Its leadership is failing to lead

20. I have been most frustrated with church when . . .
    a. I haven't found my place there
    b. We aren't doing anything
    c. People are fighting and gossiping
    d. The pastor isn't helping me grow

21. The kind of pastor who would be best for us . . .
    a. Nurtures our gifts and empowers us to serve
    b. Is a go-getter who inspires us to work for Jesus
    c. Loves us deeply and is present in our lives
    d. Is a great teacher and preacher of the word

22. The best way to share Jesus with others is to . . .
    a. Help them understand that they are special to God and God has a purpose for their lives
    b. Show them Jesus by talking the talk and walking the walk
    c. Love them and help them see God in their own lives
    d. Teach them about Jesus in a personal way

Thank you for completing the Gospel Discipleship Assessment. If you take this assessment online at www.MinistryMatters.com/gospel discipleship, your score and Gospel Discipleship type can be emailed to you.

To score this assessment on your own, tally up how many times you answered *a*, how many times you answered *b*, how many times you answered *c*, and how many times you answered *d*. Whichever letter you have the most answers for is your primary type. Your second highest score is your secondary type. You may have a tie as well, in which case you share characteristics of both types. The letters each correspond to the following types:

- A = Markan
- B = Matthean
- C = Lukan
- D = Johannine

VIDEO DESCRIPTIONS FOR GOSPEL DISCIPLESHIP

Session 1—Gospel Discipleship: The Journey Begins

Rev. Andrea Cummings meets with Gospel Discipleship author Michelle J. Morris to learn the results of her Gospel Discipleship assessment. After hearing more about Gospel Discipleship overall and how it helps in a journey of growing in faith in Christ, Andrea learns that she scored as a tie in all four types. Michelle sets Andrea off on a journey to discover what discipleship type is resonating with her at this moment in her life.

Session 2—Gospel Discipleship: Markan

Andrea's first stop on her discipleship journey takes her to the beautiful sanctuary of Argenta United Methodist Church where she meets Rev. James Kjorlaug and Bryan Ayres, two Markans. They explore with Andrea what it is like to be motivated by the active and creative presence of the Holy Spirit in directing their paths.

Session 3—Gospel Discipleship: Matthean

Andrea winds her way into the FANN (Friends and Neighbors Network) food pantry at First United Methodist Church of Little Rock to meet Samantha Black and Shelley McCarty, two Matthean disciples. These women are motivated to put their hands and feet in action to express and grow in their faith in Christ.

Session 4—Gospel Discipleship: Lukan

Andrea is welcomed into the home of Cathy Hall for the next step in her journey. Cathy and Rev. Paul Atkins, two Lukans, share stories from their lives and ministries that invite Andrea to experience relational discipleship.

Session 5—Gospel Discipleship: Johannine

Andrea steps into the University of Arkansas at Little Rock Wesley Foundation to learn more about Johannine discipleship. Rev. Trinette Barnes and Rev. Doug Phillips teach Andrea about understanding the role of mentoring in discipleship.

Session 6—Gospel Discipleship: The Journey's Next Step

Andrea reflects on the journey she has undertaken to meet people of each type. She shares what resonated with her about each of the paths before her. Then, she chooses which path makes sense for her next step in walking a life with Christ.

CPSIA information can be obtained
at www.ICGtesting.com
Printed in the USA
LVHW031926250720
661519LV00008B/9